# DevOps: A Journey from Microservice to Cloud Based Containerization

# RIVER PUBLISHERS SERIES IN COMPUTING AND INFORMATION SCIENCE AND TECHNOLOGY

*Series Editors*

**K.C. CHEN**
*National Taiwan University,*
*Taipei, Taiwan*

*University of South Florida,*
*USA*

**SANDEEP SHUKLA**
*Virginia Tech,*
*USA*

*Indian Institute of Technology Kanpur,*
*India*

The "River Publishers Series in Computing and Information Science and Technology" covers research which ushers the 21st Century into an Internet and multimedia era. Networking suggests transportation of such multimedia contents among nodes in communication and/or computer networks, to facilitate the ultimate Internet.

Theory, technologies, protocols and standards, applications/services, practice and implementation of wired/wireless

The "River Publishers Series in Computing and Information Science and Technology" covers research which ushers the 21st Century into an Internet and multimedia era. Networking suggests transportation of such multimedia contents among nodes in communication and/or computer networks, to facilitate the ultimate Internet.

Theory, technologies, protocols and standards, applications/services, practice and implementation of wired/wireless networking are all within the scope of this series. Based on network and communication science, we further extend the scope for 21st Century life through the knowledge in machine learning, embedded systems, cognitive science, pattern recognition, quantum/biological/ molecular computation and information processing, user behaviors and interface, and applications across healthcare and society.

Books published in the series include research monographs, edited volumes, handbooks and textbooks. The books provide professionals, researchers, educators, and advanced students in the field with an invaluable insight into the latest research and developments.

Topics included in the series are as follows:-

- Artificial Intelligence
- Cognitive Science and Brian Science
- Communication/Computer Networking Technologies and Applications
- Computation and Information Processing
- Computer Architectures
- Computer Networks
- Computer Science
- Embedded Systems
- Evolutionary Computation
- Information Modelling
- Information Theory
- Machine Intelligence
- Neural Computing and Machine Learning
- Parallel and Distributed Systems
- Programming Languages
- Reconfigurable Computing
- Research Informatics
- Soft Computing Techniques
- Software Development
- Software Engineering
- Software Maintenance

For a list of other books in this series, visit www.riverpublishers.com

# DevOps: A Journey from Microservice to Cloud Based Containerization

**Hitesh Kumar Sharma**

University of Petroleum and Energy Studies, Dehradun, India

**Anuj Kumar**

University of Petroleum and Energy Studies, Dehradun, India

**Sangeeta Pant**

Dev Bhoomi Uttarakhand University, Dehradun, India

**Mangey Ram**

Graphic Era Deemed to be University, Dehradun, India

NEW YORK AND LONDON

**Published 2023 by River Publishers**
River Publishers
Alsbjergvej 10, 9260 Gistrup, Denmark
www.riverpublishers.com

**Distributed exclusively by Routledge**
605 Third Avenue, New York, NY 10017, USA
4 Park Square, Milton Park, Abingdon, Oxon OX14 4RN

*DevOps: A Journey from Microservice to Cloud Based Containerization / Hitesh Kumar Sharma, Anuj Kumar, Sangeeta Pant and Mangey Ram.*

©2023 River Publishers. All rights reserved. No part of this publication may be reproduced, stored in a retrieval systems, or transmitted in any form or by any means, mechanical, photocopying, recording or otherwise, without prior written permission of the publishers.

Routledge is an imprint of the Taylor & Francis Group, an informa business

ISBN 978-87-7022-846-6 (hardback)
ISBN 978-87-7004-047-1 (paperback)
ISBN 978-10-0380-772-8 (online)
ISBN 978-1-032-62431-0 (ebook master)

While every effort is made to provide dependable information, the publisher, authors, and editors cannot be held responsible for any errors or omissions.

# Contents

# Preface

This book is motivated by the fact that transitioning to DevOps requires a change in culture and mindset. At its simplest, DevOps is about removing the barriers between two traditionally siloed teams, development and operations. In some organisations, there may not even be separate development and operations teams; engineers may do both. With DevOps, the two teams work together to optimise both the productivity of developers and the reliability of operations.

The objective of this book is to equip beginners as well as advanced readers related to DevOps with related knowledge. Here, we have emphasised introducing the DevOps culture and related tools and techniques under a techno-cultural umbrella. We have explained the microservice, containers, Dockers, etc., and the significance of these in adopting DevOps culture for successful software development.

Assoc. Prof. Dr. Hitesh Kumar Sharma
Assoc. Prof. Dr. Anuj Kumar
Assoc. Prof. Dr. Sangeeta Pant
Prof. Dr. Mangey Ram

# List of Figures

# List of Table

# List of Abbreviations

| | |
|---|---|
| **ACI** | Azure container instances |
| **AD** | Active directory |
| **AKA** | Also Known As |
| **AKS** | Azure Kubernetes services |
| **AMQP** | Advanced Message Queuing Protocol |
| **API** | Application programming interface |
| **ASF** | Azure Service Fabric |
| **AWS** | Amazon Web Services |
| **BDD** | Behaviour- Driven Development |
| **CaaS** | Containers as a Service |
| **CD** | Continuous delivery |
| **CDN** | Content delivery network |
| **CI** | Continuous integration |
| **CICD** | Continuous integration and continuous development |
| **CNCF** | Cloud Native Computing Foundation |
| **CNI** | Container network interface |
| **CSS** | Cascading Style Sheet |
| **DDD** | Domain-driven design |
| **GCP** | Google cloud platform |
| **GKE** | Google Kubernetes Engine |
| **GUI** | Graphical user interface |
| **HTML** | Hypertext Markup Language |
| **IaaS** | Infrastructure as a service |
| **IT** | Information Technology |
| **KaaS** | Kubernetes as a Service |
| **MSA** | Microservice architecture |
| **MTTR** | Mean time to recovery |
| **MVP** | Minimum Viable Product |
| **PaaS** | Platform-as-a-service |
| **PDC** | Professional Developers Conference |
| **QA** | Quality Assurance |

| | |
|---|---|
| **RDBMS** | Relational Database Management System |
| **REST** | Representational State Transfer |
| **SaaS** | Software as a service |
| **SDLC** | Software development lifecycle |
| **SOA** | Service-oriented architecture |
| **SSL** | Secure Sockets Layer |
| **UI** | User Interface |
| **V/S** | Versus |
| **VCS** | Version Control System |
| **VMs** | Virtual machines |
| **VPC** | Virtual private cloud |
| **XML** | Extensible Markup Language |
| **ZRS** | Zone redundant storage |

# 1

# DevOps: An Introduction

## Abstract

DevOps culture emphasises bringing different teams who might have different goals and thought processes together. This is considered a necessity as the end goal of each team is the same, which is to deliver a finished product on time as per the customer's requirements. DevOps culture helps in aligning the focus of everyone with the common goal. At the heart of DevOps lies transparency and full collaboration as well as communication with each team instead of working in silos. It also promotes the idea of continuous integration, improvement and learning while building trust and collaboration with the teams.

In this chapter, we have described the requirement of DevOps culture and the role of DevOps in software development process automation. A detailed description of the DevOps mindset is provided in this chapter.

## 1.1 Introduction

DevOps culture is being adopted by many unicorns of the IT sector as they believe it is the most appropriate way to increase the productivity of the company and create profit. One of the ways this is achieved is by making responsibilities shared by every team. That is if there is any failure or error in the product, the entire teams (both Development and Operations teams) are responsible instead of playing the blame game. On the other hand, on the success of the product, both teams are equally praised. When they realise the challenges faced by operations, they simplify deployment and maintenance. Likewise, when operations understand the system's business goals, they work with developers to help in defining the operational needs of a system and adopt automation tools. This naturally increases collaboration and stops the blame game thus reducing conflicts between Development and Operations teams [1, 2]. The teams are trusted to make and approve their own decisions without waiting for a lengthy period of time for formal approval. This makes the implementation of new ideas easier and encourages innovation. Frequent feedback is also required for the implementation of the DevOps culture as it helps in the continuous integration of the development process. The faster the feedback is delivered in the early stages of development the easier it is to fix the flaws or even add new features to the software. In an environment where the development and operations teams are in isolated silos, feedback about the performance and stability of application software in production is often slow to make it back to the development team, if it makes it at all. DevOps ensures that developers get the fast feedback they need to rapidly iterate and improve on application code by requiring collaboration between operations folks in designing and implementing application monitoring and reporting strategies.

The use of automation tools is also important in the DevOps culture [3]. Automation tools make the development process much faster and more streamlined while reducing human intervention.

- **Identifying and fixing errors:** Automation tools are essential to find errors using automatic testing tools like Selenium and fix them as soon as possible. This is part of the continuous integration in the DevOps culture.
- **Collaboration:** In a development environment, multiple developers work on the same source code; so it is important to maintain a level of communication and collaboration. Tools like GitHub [4] and JIRA [5] help to achieve this goal.
- **Deployment:** The goal of DevOps is to deploy a well-defined culture and functioning in the production environment. As soon as the product is ready and well-tested, it is sent for immediate delivery, and this is known as continuous delivery and continuous deployment. Docker [6] is widely used for implementing this.

While automation tools are a core of the culture, we cannot just implement tools and call it DevOps culture. DevOps culture requires a complete shift from traditional methods and requires an individual change in the perception of teams, trust and transparency.

## 1.2 DevOps: A Culture

In the 1990s, software developers began adopting lean manufacturing practices. Lean manufacturing originated in the Japanese manufacturing industry shortly after World War II and aims to increase cost, quality and delivery time by eliminating waste from the process. In 2001, the Software Development Expert Group gave up a traditional approach and tilted people, and had time to respond to customers and respond to changes. As a result of the meeting, a flexible declaration was a joint effort of 17 experts [7]. This change in agility was a great spot in the history of software development since the project was removed. In addition to this change, technological improvements are highly likely to be part of the project and provide feedback with IT teams and real-time interactions. This change led to the expiration of project management efficiency, which has been hugging the rare and rapid practice that the IT community needs to be adopted. However, all organisations still had well-known problems. It was the gap between the development team and the operations team. DevOps has emerged to bridge this gap and create synergies between teams. This methodology stems from a combination of lean and agile principles. Lean, agile, and DevOps focus on organisational culture, building interdisciplinary teams, reducing waste, customer focus, embracing change, and delivering value continuously. These methodologies emerged at different times to meet different requirements [7, 8].

## 1.3 DevOps Environment

A DevOps environment ambition is to address the difficulties by growing how well the IT operations and development team gathers work to lay out an environment depicted by a bound together, gathering with a multidisciplinary scope of capacities. This development fundamentally alters the way that gatherings collaborate and how writing computer programs functions by conquering any issues among ‘dev’ and ‘activities’ and applying strong DevOps instruments to soothe data storage facilities. Largely, a DevOps environment grows detectable quality to reduce the bet of weakness, further creates goof and bug acknowledgement, and mitigates bottlenecks and waste in the improved communication. The DevOps environment is created as a reaction against a part of the typical issues that the IT business faces, including the destroying of associates and the work they do, the weakness of introducing new features or sending changes, the difficulty of finding and tending to flees and the rising of bottlenecks inside the software development lifecycle (SDLC) [9, 10] (Figure 1.1). Relationships without a DevOps environment much of the time have a gathering structure considering a division of work. These gatherings many a time work in storage facilities, with designers, analyzers and IT action specialists working in discrete universes to achieve their singular goals. This division of work is an old model to structure bunches

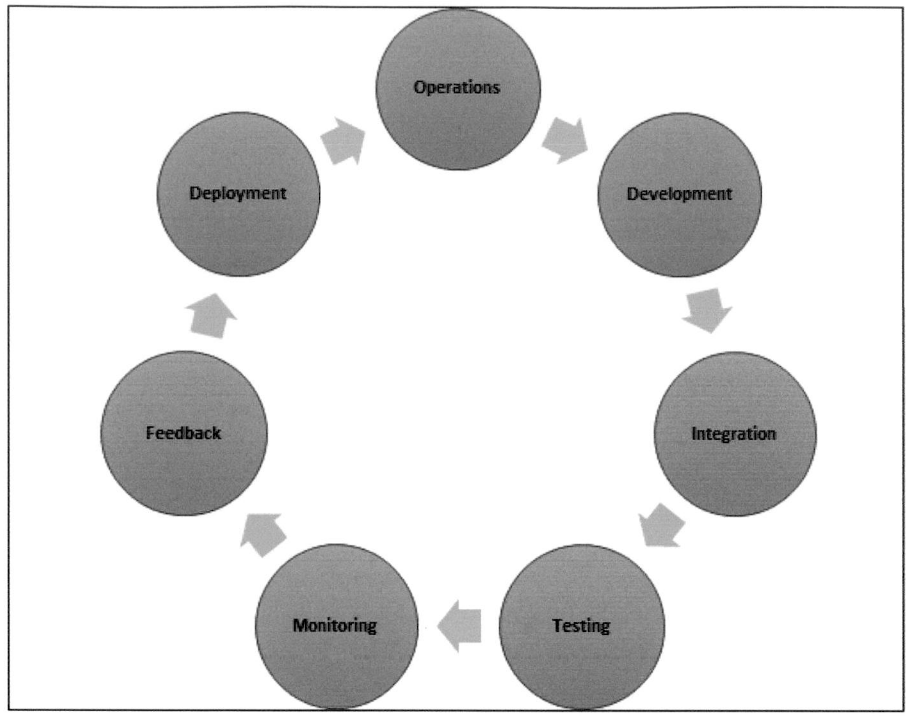


**Figure 1.1** Software development workflow.

since it makes preventions among them and obstructs their correspondence and the way wherein, they work. Accordingly, this model genuinely thwarts both deftness and speed.

A DevOps environment attempts to mitigate such troubles and various issues that could emerge on account of this model. This is done through various deals including:

- **Continuous development:** Continuous development involves coding the software and breaking the whole software into smaller different pieces [11]. This makes it easier for the DevOps team to accelerate the overall software development process. This phase is instrumental in mapping the perception of the entire development lifecycle.
- **Continuous integration:** Continuous integration is a DevOps programming improvement practice where designs regularly mix their code changes into a central store, after which automated development and tests are run.

- **Continuous testing:** This refers to the process of testing the new update within the source code as we make it. The developed code is tested for bugs and errors that may have entered the code while we were making it. Automation tools, such as selenium, TestNG, Junit, etc., are used for test automation.
- **Continuous delivery:** Deploying and conveying changes and fixes step by step in a controlled, fast way. Continuous delivery is a framework wherein the headway bunches ensure that the item is trustworthy to convey at whatever point. Everytime, every item goes through the robotised testing process. If it successfully passes the testing, it should be ready for release.
- **Continuous monitoring:** Through this step, developers identify the grey areas of the app that requires more effort for development.

A DevOps environment increases detectable quality and diminishes weakness, yet furthermore chips away at the most well-known approach to perceiving and tending to goofs, bugs and various issues [12–14]. As referred to as of now, in a DevOps environment, bunches embrace various deals including continuous integration. Through continuous integration, a DevOps environment makes a model taking into account upheld and second analysis. Gatherings can then disentangle slip-ups or bugs and address them extensively more actually than in a traditional environment, where tremendous mass changes tangle the software development cooperation and make it difficult to determine what the issue is, where it is found and who is liable for it. A DevOps environment is the key to laying out a cooperative environment that increases detectable quality, diminishes weakness and further creates a botch area. In any case, this environment helps with directing bottlenecks and killing waste in development cooperation.

## 1.4 Benefits of DevOps Culture

According to the book 'Accelerate: Building and Scaling High Performing Technology Organisations', a DevOps culture stimulates high levels of trust and collaboration, resulting in higher quality decision-making and even higher levels of job satisfaction [15].

**Key benefits of DevOps culture are:**

- Ensuring faster development
- Balancing in the workplace

- Improved Quality
- Room for innovation
- Supports agility
- Continuous Delivery of the product
- Dependable problem-solving techniques
- Transparency
- Cost Efficient
- Better manage unplanned work

### 1.4.1 Ensuring faster development

Quick and successive delivery of the product not only keeps the client satisfied but will also help the company to take a firm stand in the ongoing competitive market.

### 1.4.2 Balancing in the workplace

Do you have at least some ideas that the pressure associated with the arrival of new elements and fixes or updates can bring down the steadiness of your work area and diminishes the general efficiency? Further, develop your workplace with a consistent and even methodology of activity with DevOps practice [16, 17].

### 1.4.3 Improved quality

In DevOps culture the collaboration of the development team and operation team using user feedback play a big role in the frequent improvement in the quality of the product.

### 1.4.4 Room for innovation

Automation in repetitive tasks leaves the team with extra time in framing new ideas. In comparison to the traditional methods where it is difficult to beat the deadline in time, DevOps leaves the team with extra time for innovation.

### 1.4.5 Supports agility

It is no new thing that making your company agile can help you to be superior in this competitive market. In DevOps culture, it is currently conceivable to gain the versatility expected to change the business.

### 1.4.6 Continuous delivery of the product

All the departments are responsible for the stability and establishment of new features. So, the momentum of software is fast and undisturbed, whereas in a traditional method, the delivery part is burdened on a single team.

### 1.4.7 Dependable problem-solving techniques

Through continuous testing, it is easier to find and solve the problem. Guaranteeing speedy and stable answers for specialised blunders in programming the executives is one of the essential advantages of DevOps [17].

### 1.4.8 Transparency

The promotion of collaboration and scrum meetings allows for better and easy communication among the team members which leads to an uprise in the productivity and efficiency of the company's employees.

### 1.4.9 Cost efficient

With legitimate collaboration, DevOps helps in chopping down the administration and creation expenses of your specialisations, as both upkeep and new updates are brought under a more extensive single roof.

### 1.4.10 Better manage unplanned work

Teams who completely embrace DevOps rehearses work sharper and quicker, and convey better quality to their clients. The expanded utilisation of robotisation and cross-useful cooperation decreases intricacy and blunders, which in turn works on the mean time to recovery (MTTR) [18] when occurrences and blackouts happen.

## 1.5 Best Practices of DevOps Culture

- Project management with agility
- Shift left with CI/CD
- Using the right tools
- Implementing Automation
- Monitor the CI/CD pipeline

- Gather continuous feedback
- Cultural change

### 1.5.1 Project management with agility

Agile is an iterative way to deal with project management and software advancement that assists teams with conveying worth to their clients quickly and with less headache. Agile teams centre around conveying work in more modest augmentations, rather than sitting tight for a solo monstrous delivery date. Prerequisites, plans, and results are assessed consistently, permitting groups to answer criticism and turn as the need should arise.

### 1.5.2 Shift left with CI/CD

What happens in this is that teams bring testing into their code development in the early process instead of providing multiple changes to separate test or QA teams. This ensures that a large number of tests are performed throughout the coding process so developers can fix bugs and improve code quality when they are working on the same sort of code base. The act of continuous integration and continuous delivery (CI/CD) [19], and sending supports the capacity to move left.

### 1.5.3 Using the right tools

One of the fundamental mainstays of DevOps is automation. To empower automation and receive the most extreme advantage in return one requires the right toolchain. Allow us to take a gander at the most famous DevOps tools:

- **Jenkins**: Open-source CI/CD automation server, which helps to test, build and deploy with the help of a single tool.
- **Git**: The VCS makes the code available to the whole team anytime.
- **Selenium**: Use to write test scripts and to test web application.
- **Docker**: Open-source technology to containerise. Convert the application to a package so that it can be used on any platform.
- **Nagios**: Open-source monitoring tool.
- **Kubernetes**: Open-source cluster-orchestrator to manage the real-time container workloads.

### 1.5.4 Implementing automation

Traditionally, the automation cycle would come in the image just during the testing stage. The QA group would automate the experiments to check the code's usefulness and the Ops group would physically design the server prerequisites. That was basically the situation, however, DevOps utilises automation right from the time the code gets checked in. The code building, running the experiments, and lastly delivering the code for discharge happens consequently. That is how the whole lifecycle of DevOps is automated.

### 1.5.5 Monitor the CI/CD pipeline

Monitoring these metrics is also important because it allows you to detect when things go wrong so you can recover quickly. The DevOps metrics you track will depend on your organisation's goals and expectations. Some metrics, such as unit cost, are useful to any engineering team because they are tied to profitability. Monitoring unit cost as a DevOps metric is a good practice because it helps you build cost-optimised software from the get-go. This is because you get early insight into what your costs are so you can plan your projects and make trade-offs proactively.

### 1.5.6 Gather continuous feedback

DevOps is tied in with adopting a client-driven strategy and empowering something similar, while feedback from end-clients is fundamental. The best way to tackle this issue is to focus on client prerequisites and overcome any issues between end clients and DevOps.

### 1.5.7 Cultural change

DevOps requires collaboration, straightforwardness, trust, and sympathy. If your association is one of the uncommon ones where these characteristics are now settled, it ought to be genuinely simple for your groups to take on DevOps rehearses. If not, some work will be expected to foster these characteristics. The most widely recognised hierarchical designs are siloed, meaning various groups have separate areas of possession and obligation and there is insignificant cross-group correspondence or cooperation. For DevOps to succeed, these obstructions should be wiped out by embracing the 'you construct it, you run it' practice. This does not mean there are not individuals or groups who practice, just that the lines of correspondence and cooperation between groups are open and utilised.

## 1.6 Challenges in DevOps Culture

There any many challenges faced by an organisation while inheriting the DevOps culture in their software development lifecycle.

Some of the challenges are as follows.

### 1.6.1 Overcoming the mentality of Dev V/S Ops

In numerous associations, we can see the old tradition of designers throwing code over a non-existent divider to a brought-together activities group where engineers are attempting to advance and make changes as fast as could really be expected, and the tasks group are attempting to keep up with high assistance levels. The targets of these two gatherings frequently counter one another, causing grating focuses and bringing about handovers and expanded costs, alongside longer input circles. DevOps is tied in with coordinating groups together and separating storehouses inside IT associations. This outing begins by setting out a fantasy on how this will work for your affiliation. Getting jobs and obligations of where the development team stops and operations at present begins, and how these can best be incorporated together, is an extraordinary beginning stage for any particular organisation, and it is generally expected the principal obstacle that it needs to defeat as it takes on DevOps rehearses.

### 1.6.2 Ordinary understanding of continuous-delivery practices in an organisation

At the point when you have recognised that your code ought to be continually passed on to restrict input circles, and your experts have executed pipelines and CI tooling that engage you to do this, you truly need to present yourself with this request. Do your part bunches genuinely fathom what it means to reliably convey your item into your environmental elements and at a more essential repeat? Most affiliations will have their own significance regarding what continuous delivery means for them. All things considered, we describe continuous movement as a lot of cycles that grant you to constantly and financially release new programming changes of different kinds (new features, bug fixes, etc.) by ensuring that your architects' movements never split the guideline project-staying aware of it in a reliably deployable state. The communication licenses you to make sure that your full errand is in a valuable, clean state, preceding shipping off the creation environment. Giving unquestionable importance to continuous delivery for your affiliation can help in spreading out a normal perception of what it means to constantly pass and how to achieve security.

### 1.6.3 Moving on to microservices from legacy infrastructure and architecture

More seasoned foundations and applications having complex design stacks can become dangerous, regardless of whether they have served the organisation for quite a long time. Staying aware of the standard can routinely incite adequacy issues, nonappearance of help and high practical costs – all finally achieving being left behind the resistance. Including the establishment of as-code alongside microservices designing is a huge development towards a possible destiny of predictable turn of events, which results in clearly rethinking and modernising the entire programming improvement lifecycle and grants the business to quickly acclimate to changing business areas and client needs. Moving towards a more cloud-neighbourhood natural framework with microservices designing can open up the courses to faster progression and speedier turn of events. In addition, it is key to have a solid foundation around robotisation, plan the board and consistent transport practices to adjust to an extended useful obligation that microservices bring.

### 1.6.4 Implementing the strategy of test automation

Your affiliation most certainly understands that mechanised tests are genuinely critical and are a key engaging specialist for DevOps chips away at including CI/CD. So what is ending the respite on test motorisation? It is not just about getting out anything the test strategy is, yet also doing an amazing job with the test execution of that system as a coordinating north star for the gatherings. This joins things like BDD practices and the three-amigo approach, as well as answering key requests, for instance.

- How might we do data on the board for our tests?
- Could we have the option to use freely delivered shared libraries and typical practices?
- What does a nice beginning-to-end test look like for our code base?
- What should our smoke tests genuinely do?

Having a sensible understanding of how to complete the test strategy can go far in getting test robotisation taken on across the more broad affiliation, shortening the info circles and getting your things out the doorway speedier.

### 1.6.5 Emphasising more on tools

With the intriguing chance of embracing DevOps, flashy new gadgets in the market can seem like they tackle each issue under the sun. Regardless, with the introduction of new instruments comes the need to set up your staff on the most ideal way to use them. Ensuring they meet security requirements and are specially organised with the current system [20, 21]. This can divert you from your key need: your gathering. Your gathering and your association structure are basic to DevOps. At the point when you have the right development set-up, the patterns of the gathering will follow. Likewise, when the cycles are portrayed, then, you can choose the devices expected to meet the cycles. People in your gathering are the fundamental component while changing to DevOps.

In affiliations where DevOps practices are being done, we really see that gatherings do not have full liability regarding a course of action and conveyance examples of their item. This is frequently because of the absence of comprehension of the distinction between conveying and delivering. Conveying is your product being introduced, in a manner of speaking, into any climate, including dev, test or push. Delivering is then moving forward, and making it accessible to the end client. This is significant so the full cross-useful group idea of 'you fabricate, you run it' can be executed appropriately. A good way to deal with this is for the gathering to start working personally with any tasks individuals and accepting a feeling of pride with associations, conveyances and exercises, so there is a split setting between the two. This licenses devs, for instance, to identify with activities bunches on the stuff to truly send and convey their code in progress. Having this setting can help in embracing DevOps practices for the entire gathering, and can engage the gathering to start taking more time for just associations, yet also conveys!

### 1.6.6 Resistance to new change

The progress to DevOps can give off an impression of being disturbing to a couple of associates and key accomplices. Packaging it as a progression of current improvement practices as opposed to a change can help that issue. Encouraging people that they need to change ought to be apparent as a horrendous reflection on the individual getting the direction. It should be focused on that a DevOps change does not happen suddenly; it ought to be smooth and slow. This licenses everyone to embrace the DevOps culture as they continuously become familiar with it and comprehend the different ways, they can add to the headway cooperation.

A nice approach is to notice a little thing or full-stack slice of a current application to upgrade it into DevOps practices. This will reliably work with the sensation of freshness, and get everyone on board to enter the new universe of DevOps.

### 1.6.7 Dev and Ops toolset conflicts

It can in like manner be an issue when dev and activities bunches have entirely unexpected toolsets and estimations. As essential as it would show up, it is beneficial to put the two gatherings down and hope to understand where it is really smart to organise the instruments they use, and unite the estimations they screen. A couple of gatherings may be hesitant to leave behind imaginatively average legacy devices, yet what is more deferred down the entire system due to similitude issues. Guarantee the contraptions that are being completed are agreed with the targets of the association and do not possess from your basic objective. Vanquishing these fundamental challenges, to begin with, will make the move to DevOps much smoother. All through some time interval, every partner will become familiar with the vibe of reliable change and headway. Once the dev, activities and various gatherings sort out some way to partake, they will choose ways to deal with supporting each other, and cooperating altogether more eagerly.

## 1.7 Conclusion

Interest can be a strong motivation for some to start learning! By far, one of the fundamental enabling impacts for the gathering to start embracing a DevOps mentality is the interest to constantly learn, change and work on their capacities and data. One way to deal with achieving this is by ensuring that there is a phase that is available for gatherings to enable learning and sharing. This can be through organisations of practices where the affiliation places assets into a day of learning and data sharing one time every month, through lunch and learn gatherings, or embracing social orders across gatherings. Moreover, a train-the-mentor model can in like manner be executed to ensure that practices are shared across all of the gatherings, paying little psyche to how enormous or minimal the affiliation is. A culture of interminable learning, paying little heed to which approach you take, can be the underlying minimal development that changes into a significant leap in embracing DevOps practices.

## References

[1] Fitzgerald, B. and Stol, K.-J. Continuous software engineering: A roadmap and agenda. Journal of Systems and Software, 123 (2017), 176–189.

[2] K. Kustwar, and R. Suman. (2020). 'E-Health and telemedicine in India: An overview on the health care need of the people.' Journal of Multidisciplinary Research in Healthcare, 6(2), 25–36. https://doi.org/10.15415/jmrh.2020.62004.

[3] Priyanka, T. K., Singh, M. K., & Kumar, A. (2022). Deep learning for satellite-based data analysis. Meta-heuristic Optimization Techniques: Applications in Engineering, 10, 173.

[4] Pant, S., Kumar, A., Ram, M., Klochkov, Y., & Sharma, H. K. (2022). Consistency Indices in Analytic Hierarchy Process: A Review. Mathematics, 10(8), 1206.

[5] Uniyal, N., Pant, S., Kumar, A., & Pant, P. (2022). Nature-inspired metaheuristic algorithms for optimization. Meta-heuristic Optimization Techniques: Applications in Engineering, 10, 1.

[6] Khanchi, Ishu, Ezaz Ahmed, and Hitesh Kumar Sharma. "Automated framework for real-time sentiment analysis." 5th International Conference on Next Generation Computing Technologies (NGCT-2019). 2020.

[7] H. K. Sharma, R. Tomar, A. Dumka and M. S. Aswal, "OpenECOCOMO: The algorithms and implementation of Extended Cost Constructive Model (E-COCOMO)," 2015 1st International Conference on Next Generation Computing Technologies (NGCT), 2015, pp. 773–778, doi: 10.1109/NGCT.2015.7375225.

[8] Sharma, Hitesh KUMAR. "E-COCOMO: the extended cost constructive model for cleanroom software engineering." Database Systems Journal 4.4 (2013): 3–11.

[9] Sharma, Hitesh Kumar, et al. "Real time activity logger: a user activity detection system." Int J Eng Adv Technol 9.1 (2019): 1991–1994.

[10] Taneja, Sahil, et al. "AirBits: A Web Application Development using Microsoft Azure." ICRDSTHM-17) Kuala Lumpur, Malaysia (2017).

[11] H. K. Sharma, S. Kumar, S. Dubey and P. Gupta, "Auto-selection and management of dynamic SGA parameters in RDBMS," 2015 2nd International Conference on Computing for Sustainable Global Development (INDIACom), 2015, pp. 1763–1768.

[12] Sharma, Hitesh KUMAR, Sanjeev KUMAR Singh, and Prashant Ahlawat. "Model-based testing: the new revolution in software testing." Database Syst J 4.1 (2014): 26–31.

[13] Sharma, Hitesh Kumar, et al. "SGA Dynamic Parameters: The Core Components of Automated Database Tuning." Database Systems Journal 5.2 (2014): 13–21.

[14] Sharma, Hitesh Kumar, et al. "An effective model of effort estimation for Cleanroom software development approach." ICRDSTHM-17) Kuala Lumpur, Malasyia (2017).

[15] Singh, Himmat, Aman Jatain, and Hitesh Kumar Sharma. "A review on search based software engineering." IJRIT Int. J. Res. Inform. Technol 2.4 (2014).

[16] Kumar, A., Pant, S., Ram, M., & Yadav, O. (Eds.). (2022). Meta-heuristic Optimization Techniques: Applications in Engineering (Vol. 10). Walter de Gruyter GmbH & Co KG.

[17] Sharma, Hitesh Kumar, et al. "Sensors based smart healthcare framework using internet of things (IoT)." International Journal of Scientific and Technology Research 9.2 (2020): 1228–1234.

[18] Tiwari, Rajeev, et al. "Automated parking system-cloud and IoT based technique." International Journal of Engineering and Advanced Technology (IJEAT) 8.4C (2019): 116–123.

[19] Sharma, Hitesh Kumar, et al. "I-Doctor: An IoT based self patient's health monitoring system." 2019 International Conference on Innovative Sustainable Computational Technologies (CISCT). IEEE, 2019.

[20] Kumar, A., Negi, G., Pant, S., Ram, M., & Dimri, S. C. (2021). Availability-Cost Optimization of Butter Oil Processing System by Using Nature Inspired Optimization Algorithms. Reliability: Theory & Applications, (SI 2 (64)), 188–200.

[21] Kumar, A., Vohra, M., Pant, S., & Singh, S. K. (2021). Optimization techniques for petroleum engineering: A brief review. International Journal of Modelling and Simulation, 41(5), 326–334.

# 2

# Microservice versus Monolithic Architecture


## Abstract

Over the past decade, software development has been evolving rapidly to keep pace with technological advances and consumer needs. While custom development depends on one large code of codes, many applications today are built from a few applications or microservice, each of which is bound to have a single application functionality. Together they formulate a program called microservice architecture.

In this chapter, we have explained the difference between microservice and monolithic architecture-based applications. The significance of microservice-based applications in DevOps culture is described in detail in this chapter.


## 2.1 Introduction

Lately, microservices or microservice architecture is the entire buzz in developing new software applications. It has increased the popularity and use of technologies like container and container orchestration. However, this does not mean that software applications were not developed before the innovation of microservices. The large-scale application was developed even before the initiation of microservices. The old software architecture that we used before microservice architecture was monolithic architecture. In a simple sense, monolithic means made up of only one piece – a large single piece of block or stone. It is important to understand the meaning of the word monolithic before diving deep into understanding monolithic architecture. In more technical terms, a monolithic architecture is something that consists of only one piece. It is large, powerful and indivisible and is very difficult to change. An application that was built using this architecture is known as a monolithic application and has all the properties of monolithic architecture. This was a

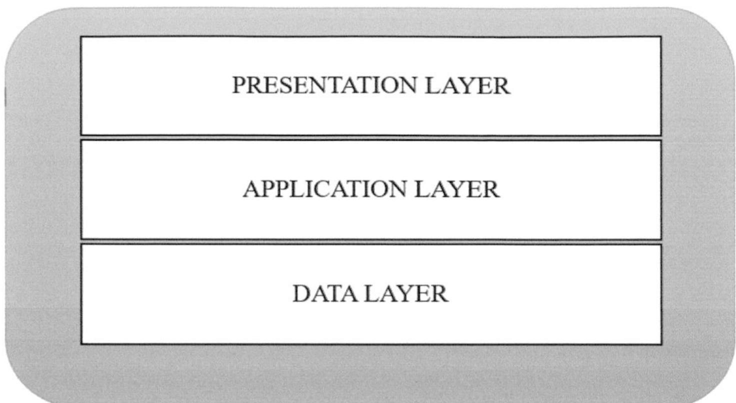


**Figure 2.1** Three-tier architecture of an application.

high-level definition of what monolithic architecture is. In the next part, we will discuss monolithic architecture in a more detailed manner.

Monolithic architecture is the traditional architecture to build application software. In this architecture, all the components or parts of the system are unified together just like the meaning of the word monolithic [1].

The application software that is built and deployed through monolithic architecture is designed in a way such that it is self-contained. That means all the components, which make up the application software are packed and deployed together as a one single unit. To understand it better, let us assume that there is a big container and all the components of the application software are tightly packed together inside this big container and deployed as one single piece. If the software is developed using Java programming language, then this container can be JAR, WAR or EAR [2, 3]. Since various components are packed together, they are interconnected and interdependent on each other, unlike software that is developed in a modular way. It has its own sets of advantages and disadvantages which we will discuss in the later part. Primarily three layers are packed together in an application software developed using monolithic architecture. These layers are the presentation layer at the top, underneath which we have the application layer and at the very bottom we have the data layer (Figure 2.1).

- **Presentation layer:** Basically, the upper layer, which is the presentation layer, is the front end of the software. A user interacts with the application through the user interface. In software that is deployed on the web server, this presentation layer is made using web technologies like HTML (Hypertext Markup Language), CSS (Cascading Style

Sheet) [4], JavaScript or through various other popular web development frameworks that are available. It communicates with the other two layers using an API (application programming interface) call [5].

- **Application layer:** This is a significant layer and consists of all the business logic of the application software. This layer is usually written using Java, .NET, C#, Python or C++.
- **Data layer:** This is the final layer and acts as the storage of the application. All the data are present in this layer and to access this layer, the application layer uses API calls. This layer consists of Databases like MySQL, Oracle DB, Microsoft SQL Server, MongoDB, etc.

### 2.1.1 Monolithic architecture examples

Let us consider we are building an e-commerce platform using monolithic architecture. We will deploy this e-commerce platform as a website. The user would be able to access the website through both mobile browsers and desktop browsers. The website will allow its customer to order items from its website; the order will only be placed after checking the inventory. If the product is available, it will ask for the payment method, verify it and then ship it to the customer. The website will contain multiple components. There will be a user interface with various backend services for verifying inventory, verifying payment methods and shipping services. If we use Java to develop this e-commerce web platform, then we can package it inside a single WAR file, which we can run on a container like a Tomcat. The architecture will look something like this (Figure 2.2).

### 2.1.2 Advantages of monolithic architecture

We can all see the disadvantages of monolithic architecture and with the rise of microservices, those disadvantages are more obvious, and monolithic architecture is seen as a villain. Yet monolithic architecture has its own set of advantages. Monolithic architecture has served the IT industry for decades now and the odd thing is that in the first place, it was never a good idea, to begin with, and the idea of a modular way of development was around for decades. Yet, developers preferred monolithic architecture, but the question is why? It is very simple to answer this question; monolithic architecture is very convenient in practical use.

Microservices is all the hype but if not implemented properly can leave people and organisation disappointed [3, 4]. Blindly choosing microservices

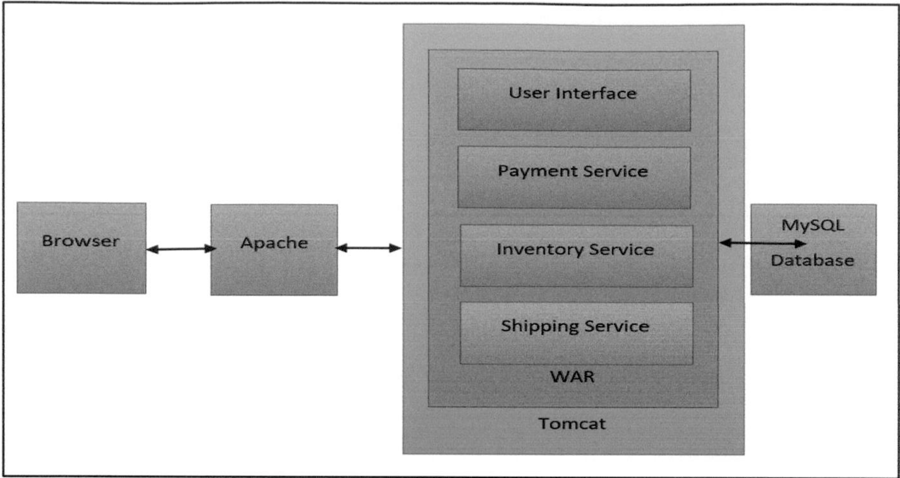


**Figure 2.2** Flow of services in three-tier architecture.

over monolithic architecture because of the buzz and not understanding the technicality can lead to complexing the problem rather than solving it.

#### 2.1.2.1 Convenience and simplicity

The monolithic architecture is very simple. It is easier to develop a software in monolithic architecture and deploy it. Since monolithic architecture has been around for decades now, most of the IDEs and software development tools are made to support monolithic architecture.

#### 2.1.2.2 Debugging and testing

Debugging and Testing is easier in monolithic architecture when compared to its counterpart. Microservices having a lot of components and multiple variables can lead to very complex software. Testing and debugging these kinds of complex systems becomes very difficult and tiresome. On the other hand, a monolithic architecture, which has all the components tightly packed inside one big container, is very easy to test and debug. There is also no issue with compatibility in monolithic systems as there are now other containers, but in microservice systems, we have to check and test the compatibility in microservices.

#### 2.1.2.3 Performance

The most important aspect of the software is its performance. Since the microservices in an application use API calls to communicate with each other, if the system is complex and has many microservices and API calls, it can lag and slow down a lot. Since monolithic architecture has one container and very few API calls it can generally give better performance results [6, 7].

### 2.1.3 Disadvantages of monolithic architecture

With the rise of new technologies and the hype around microservices, the disadvantages of monolithic architecture are quite obvious. Since these programs have a strict integration process, any changes made to the code could jeopardise the performance of the entire system. Performance was highly dependent at times in a new technological era that required continuous innovation and flexibility. Another problem with monolithic architecture was its inability to measure individual performance. One important factor for successful businesses is their ability to adapt to the needs of their customers. Naturally, these needs depend on a variety of factors and vary over time. In some cases, your business will need to limit only one activity for its service to respond to a growing number of requests. With monolithic applications, you were not able to rate individual elements but needed to rate the entire application.

#### 2.1.3.1 Large code base

The codes written in monolithic architecture are often quite large. So, when the application grows, new employees are added and since the code is so big it might scare the new developers joining the team. In addition, a very large code base has its very own problem; it is very difficult to maintain a large code base.

#### 2.1.3.2 Resistance to change

Since all the layers are tightly packed and the code base not being modular, it is very hard to change the application, even a slight change in one of the services will cause the function to misbehave and in turn, will need to be changed completely. And since changes are nearly impossible, developers are forced to use the same initial technologies even if new and better technologies are available. This means that the developers need to be motivated and dedicated to using a single development stack. Also, it is very hard to roll out frequent updates.

#### 2.1.3.3 Scalability and flexibility

It is the biggest factor in the downfall of monolithic architecture. With the internet being way more accessible than ever before, the user base is ever expanding. The demands of the user base are also very hard to predict and monolithic architecture being a change-resistant architecture is not able to handle this surge of demands. This is where new technologies like microservices and containers come to the rescue. These new technologies can efficiently allocate resources and adding new resources during surge hours also becomes very easy and efficient.

## 2.2 Microservices

We want to develop an application, what kind of architecture should we adopt? Should we go for a monolithic architecture or should we go for the microservices architecture? How should we decide which one would be good for us? These are some questions that arise when a team/organisation plans on developing any application. Directly jumping to any conclusion without a detailed discussion of both of the architectures would make no sense. The reason behind the same is that both these architectures whether it is monolithic architecture or microservices architecture have their own sets of pros and cons. It totally depends on one's needs to choose what kind of architecture they want to go for. This chapter is designed in such a way that it will make you understand what monolithic and microservices architecture really is? Some of the advantages/disadvantages of the same.

When to use what kind of architecture? Last but not the least, the most significant question is which architecture is better – monolithic or microservices? All of us might have heard that unicorns like Netflix, Apple, Google, etc., have shifted from monolithic architecture to microservices architecture [8]. Why are they doing so? Is monolithic architecture not good for developing applications anymore? There are many questions when it comes to choosing the architecture, but before answering these questions one should be very clear with the terms monolithic and microservices (Figure 2.3).

If you open a dictionary and search for the meaning of the word monolithic, you will get to know that it is basically a combination of two words namely 'mono' meaning single and 'lithic' meaning stone. Combining these terms, we can easily get to know the meaning of the term monolithic. In the software industry, monolithic refers to the development of an application where everything is present in a single code base. Usually, as a student or as a beginner, who is new to the development of applications would consider developing applications using the monolithic architecture only because it is quite simple, as you need only a single source file and a single database, which is connected to it. This is not that complex, this in turn makes it quite easy to debug, deploy and manage. On the other hand, microservices

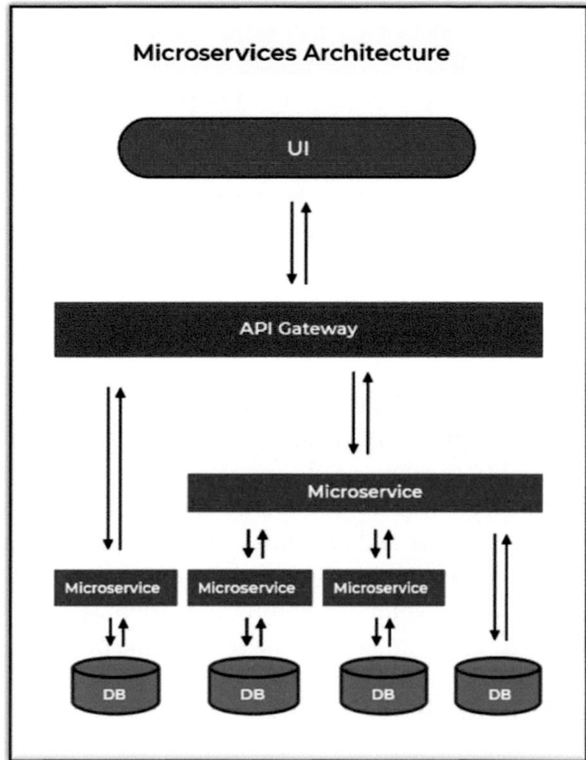


**Figure 2.3** Microservice architecture.

is completely contrary to monolithic [9]. Microservices is the combination of 'micro' meaning small and 'services'. Contrary to the monolithic architecture where the complete application is developed using a single codebase, microservices involves development of applications in small pieces/services, which in turn are independent from each other. For instance, if we consider the previous example only, now we will have multiple files and each will have its own database. Applications developed using the microservices architecture are easily scalable, independently deployable, easy to understand and also easy to expand. In the coming section of this chapter, we will dive deep into microservices, and try to understand the pros and cons of this architecture. To begin with, in the next section, let us understand monolithic architecture in brief and understand how it really works, and what are its pros and cons and then answer the question: Is the development of applications via monolithic architecture outdated and if yes, then why is it so?

### 2.2.1 Advantages of microservices architecture

#### 2.2.1.1 Easy to scale

One of the significant advantages of the microservices architecture is that it is very flexible for scaling. So, for example, if I need to scale a certain part of my application where a large number of requests are incoming so, all I need to do is scale that particular part of the application horizontally and not the complete application vertically. This is where the concept of horizontal and vertical scaling comes into action so unlike in the monolithic architecture where one needs to scale the complete application horizontally here in microservices architecture you can scale according to the needs of the end-users.

#### 2.2.1.2 Flexible choice of databases

Another significant advantage of using the microservices architecture is that you have the flexibility to choose your own databases for different microservices. So, for example, if I need a NoSQL database [10, 11] for one of my microservices, I can easily do that and can have a different SQL database [12, 13] for some different microservices. This is the flexibility that microservices architecture provides you while developing any application. Unlike that in a monolithic architecture, where you can have only one database.

#### 2.2.1.3 Flexible tech stack

While developing applications with the microservices architecture you have the flexibility to choose different tech stacks for different microservices. For example, you can develop one of your microservices using Python and another microservice using NodeJS. This indeed becomes one of the major advantages while working with a large team where different members are comfortable with different tech stacks.

#### 2.2.1.4 Minimal downtime on releases

Let us suppose that you want to release a new version of your product in the market. So in a monolithic architecture what happened was that the complete application will go through a downtime while you can deploy your updates but in a microservices architecture only that certain part of the application will go down on which you have made the changes and wish to update. This in turn creates a better user experience.

#### 2.2.1.5 Minimal chances of complete breakdown

Another significant advantage of using microservices architecture is that your complete application will not break if something goes wrong. So, let us say you have made certain changes in a part of the microservices. So if something goes wrong then it will go wrong in that particular part of microservices only and not the complete application unlike that in a monolithic architecture wherein if you have made some changes to your application and if something goes wrong the complete application will go down. This will create a bad user experience and can cost the organisation financially.

### 2.2.2 Disadvantages of microservices architecture

#### 2.2.2.1 Complex to debug

One of the major disadvantages of developing applications via the microservices architecture is that these applications are very hard to debug. Since the complete application comprises multiple microservices and one microservice might depend on another microservice to debug or test. So, for example, if you have made some changes in one of the microservices so to check that it is working fine you need to check with other microservices as well.

#### 2.2.2.2 Error handling

Another disadvantage that comes up with developing applications via a microservice architecture is that it is very hard to identify errors. Unlike the monolithic architecture wherein you can easily identify the errors as everything is present in a single code base, wherein in a microservices architecture where everything is present as a loosely coupled service independent from each other it becomes very hard to handle the errors. To check for errors, you need to dive deep into the communication between various services.

#### 2.2.2.3 Involvement of monitoring tools

Unlike the monolithic architecture wherein everything is present in a single code base and there is no need to use any kind of monitoring tool, when it comes to the microservices architecture you need to have a monitoring tool to check and monitor the logs of the various microservices. All the bugs and logs should be stored in a centralised place to check for some of the problems in the application in the future. However, this is not the case in monolithic architecture [14].

#### 2.2.2.4 Managing communication amongst microservices

As we are already familiar with the concept of the microservices architecture and we know that there are multiple microservices present. The issue that arises here is that we need to manage the communication amongst various microservices which in turn can become quite complex to manage. Some of the microservices might use synchronous commutation whereas the other microservices might use an asynchronous mode of communication. This in turn leads to an increase in the complexity of the application.

#### 2.2.2.5 Productivity issues

Yet another disadvantage of using the microservices architecture is that productivity might face a hit. To develop an application using the microservices architecture you need a team of experienced developers who are familiar with the concept of the microservices architecture. Imagine if a fresher or newbie comes into your team then it can hamper your productivity as you need to make them understand this kind of architecture. Also, if you make some changes in any of the microservices then you need to run alongside the other microservices to make sure that it is working fine.

## 2.3 Monolithic versus Microservices

Now since we are clear about what monolithic and microservices architectures really are and we are clear with some of their advantages followed by their disadvantages. Now let us rewind back to where it all started, that is, if we want to develop an application, what kind of architecture should we adopt? Should we go for a monolithic architecture or should we go for the microservices architecture? How should we decide which one will be good for us? This is the question that we started with, so are we able to answer this question? I guess yes, most of us must have realised that it is not about the architecture it is about you and the application you are developing.

Both architectures have their own set of advantages as well as disadvantages so it would not be good for you to say that one is better and the other one is not that good. Whenever you get stuck while choosing which architecture you should go forward with then you only need to answer these few simple questions and you will be good to go. These questions are as follows:

- Is the application that we are going to develop simple or complex?
- Is the size of my team big or small?
- Is my team familiar with that particular kind of architecture?
- Is scalability/zero downtime a must-have for my application?
- Is my team experienced enough and has some prior experience in this domain?
- Is my tech stack a set of multiple programming languages?

After answering these questions, you will get a better idea about the choice of architecture that you want to go forward with. For instance, let us say you are developing a complex application and then go forward with microservices else a monolithic architecture is better if your project is small [15]. Similarly, if the team size is big go with microservices else go with monolithic. If scalability is significant then choose microservices else go with the monolithic architecture. If your team is not experienced enough and you have a single programming language in your tech stack then you should go forward with the monolithic architecture else you can go forward with the microservices architecture. Last but not least we would like to conclude the article by saying that it is not the architecture that is good/bad it is about you and your team and the fact that how much comfortable you are while developing your application with that particular architecture. So, the next time you go forward to develop any application then make sure you answer the above six questions and then you will have a clear idea of which architecture you want to choose. This was all about monolithic and microservices architecture.

## 2.4 Conclusion

Over the past decade, software development has been evolving rapidly to keep pace with technological advances and consumer needs. While custom development depends on one large code of codes, many applications today are built from a few applications or microservices, each of which is bound to single application functionality. Microservices, or rather microservice architecture, is a program used to develop applications, built on a selection of unique services that work together to ensure seamless and highly responsive functionality. When you create a web application using microservice architecture, you break it down into individual tasks, develop, and execute each as a separate application. In contrast to monolithic development, where everything is integrated and, therefore, dependent on each other, the construction of a microservice consists of multiple independent modules. It is a type of structure that relies on a loose bonding system.

## References

[1] Ståhl, D. and Bosch, J. Modeling continuous integration practice differences in industry software development. Journal of Systems and Software, 87 (2014), 48–59. Hitesh Kumar Sharma; Anuj Kumar; Sangeeta Pant; Mangey Ram, "6 Application of Blockchain in Smart Healthcare," in Artificial Intelligence, Blockchain and IoT for Smart Healthcare , River Publishers, 2022, pp.57–66.

[2] Lwakatare, L. E., Kuvaja, P. and Oivo, M. Relationship of DevOps to Agile, Lean and Continuous Deployment: A Multivocal Literature Review Study. Springer, City, 2016.

[3] Kumar, A., Negi, G., Pant, S., Ram, M., & Dimri, S. C. (2021). Availability-Cost Optimization of Butter Oil Processing System by Using Nature Inspired Optimization Algorithms. Reliability: Theory & Applications, (SI 2 (64)), 188–200.

[4] H. K. Sharma, R. Tomar, A. Dumka and M. S. Aswal, "OpenECOCOMO: The algorithms and implementation of Extended Cost Constructive Model (E-COCOMO)," 2015 1st International Conference on Next Generation Computing Technologies (NGCT), 2015, pp. 773–778, doi: 10.1109/NGCT.2015.7375225.

[5] Sharma, Hitesh KUMAR. "E-COCOMO: the extended cost constructive model for cleanroom software engineering." Database Systems Journal 4.4 (2013): 3–11.

[6] Sharma, Hitesh Kumar, et al. "Real time activity logger: a user activity detection system." Int J Eng Adv Technol 9.1 (2019): 1991–1994.

[7] Priyanka, T. K., Singh, M. K., & Kumar, A. (2022). Deep learning for satellite-based data analysis. Meta-heuristic Optimization Techniques: Applications in Engineering, 10, 173.

[8] Pant, S., Kumar, A., Ram, M., Klochkov, Y., & Sharma, H. K. (2022). Consistency Indices in Analytic Hierarchy Process: A Review. Mathematics, 10(8), 1206.

[9] Uniyal, N., Pant, S., Kumar, A., & Pant, P. (2022). Nature-inspired metaheuristic algorithms for optimization. Meta-heuristic Optimization Techniques: Applications in Engineering, 10, 1.

[10] Khanchi, Ishu, Ezaz Ahmed, and Hitesh Kumar Sharma. "Automated framework for real-time sentiment analysis." 5th International Conference on Next Generation Computing Technologies (NGCT-2019). 2020.

[11] Kumar, A., Pant, S., Ram, M., & Yadav, O. (Eds.). (2022). Meta-heuristic Optimization Techniques: Applications in Engineering (Vol. 10). Walter de Gruyter GmbH & Co KG.

[12] Sharma, Hitesh Kumar, and Mr SC Nelson. "Explain Plan and SQL Trace the Two Approaches for RDBMS Tuning." Database Systems Journal BOARD (2017): 31.

[13] Sharma, Hitesh Kumar, Aditya Shastri, and Ranjit Biswas. "A Framework for Automated Database TuningUsing Dynamic SGA Parameters and Basic Operating System Utilities." Database Systems Journal 3.4 (2012): 25–32.

[14] Sharma, Hitesh Kumar, Aditya Shastri, and Ranjit Biswas. "Architecture of Automated Database Tuning Using SGA Parameters." configurations 5 (2012): 6.

[15] Sharma, Hitesh Kumar, et al. "Sensors based smart healthcare framework using internet of things (IoT)." International Journal of Scientific and Technology Research 9.2 (2020): 1228–1234.

# 3

# Implementation of Microservice


## Abstract

Microservice is used to adopt a modular approach for a software project. A single microservice is implemented for unique functionality. Implementation of individual functionality is a challenging task for the development team but the advantage received is more over the challenges faced.

In this chapter, we have explained the architecture and implementation of microservice. The platforms used for the development of microservice are also explained in detail.


## 3.1 Introduction

Microservices is a new software engineering organizational technique that is becoming increasingly widespread. Microservices' guiding philosophy is to separate an application's business components into tiny services which can be installed and run on their own. Service boundaries are described as the separation of concerns between services. Business needs and organizational hierarchy boundaries are inextricably linked to service borders. Individual services may be associated with distinct teams, budgets and timetables. Payment processing and user authentication services are two examples of service boundaries. Microservices vary from traditional software development approaches [1], which grouped all components together.

In the following section, we will use the fictional start-up Pizza Hub to demonstrate how microservices may be used by a modern software company [2].

## 3.2 Building Microservices

### 3.2.1 Create monolithic architecture

The first microservices' best practice is that you are unlikely to require them. The business demands are likely to alter often while you are constructing your MVP if your app has no users. This is related to the nature of software development, as well as the feedback loop that must occur when defining your system's important business skills must supply. Microservices do make a lot of complexities and expenses to the management process. Therefore, placing all of the code and logic in a single codebase decreases the complexity of new projects by allowing you to easily alter the borders of your application's distinct modules. For example, when we launched Pizza Hub, we may have had a straightforward idea of the problem we intended to tackle for potential consumers; we wanted customers to be capable to order pizza online. While we consider the pizza-buying problem, we will begin to see the many features that our application will need to meet that demand. We will need to keep track of a list of the different pizzas we can make, allow consumers to select one or more pizzas, process payments, schedule deliveries, and so on [3, 4]. We could conclude that allowing our clients to register an account will make it easier for them to re-order the next stint they use Pizza Hub, and after speaking with our initial users, we might discover that live delivery tracking and mobile assistance will undoubtedly give us an edge over the competition (Figure 3.1).

What began as a basic need rapidly expands into a list of skills that you must possess.

Microservices function successfully when we understand the responsibilities of the many services that your system requires. They are a lot more challenging to deal with when an application's essential needs are still being worked out. In microservices, redefining service interfaces, APIs, and data architectures are unquestionably costly since there are likely to be many more moving pieces to coordinate. This is why we recommend keeping things basic until you have gotten enough user feedback, to be confident that your consumers' basic needs are recognised and prepared for. However, developing a monolith may soon result in sophisticated code that is difficult to break down into smaller components. Try to identify as many clear modules as possible so that you may get them out of the monolith later. You may also begin by isolating your web UI from your functionality and ensuring that it communicates with the backend using the RESTful API [5] via HTTPs. When we start shifting a selection of API resources [6] to various services in the future, this will make the move to microservices easier.

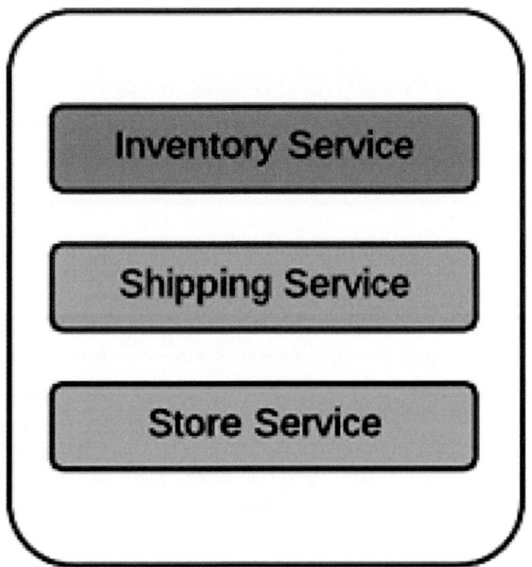


**Figure 3.1** Monolith architecture.

### 3.2.2 Organise your teams properly

Until it appeared that creating microservices was primarily a technological endeavour. You will need to break the codebase into numerous services; implement necessary failure and recovery methods, deal with data consistency, monitor service demand, and so on. There will be many new ideas to learn, but one that must not be overlooked is the necessity to reorganise your teams.

> 'Any company that creates a system will create a design that is a carbon replica of the company's communication infrastructure'.
>
> – Conway's Law.

Conway's Law is a factual phenomenon that can be witnessed in all sectors of the organization, and if a programming team is grouped with a backend crew, a frontend crew, and an operations crew separated, they can end up providing a completely separated frontend designed and backend designed monoliths that are thrown gone to the operations team to manage in production.

This arrangement is not appropriate for microservices since each service may be viewed as a separate product that must be released separately

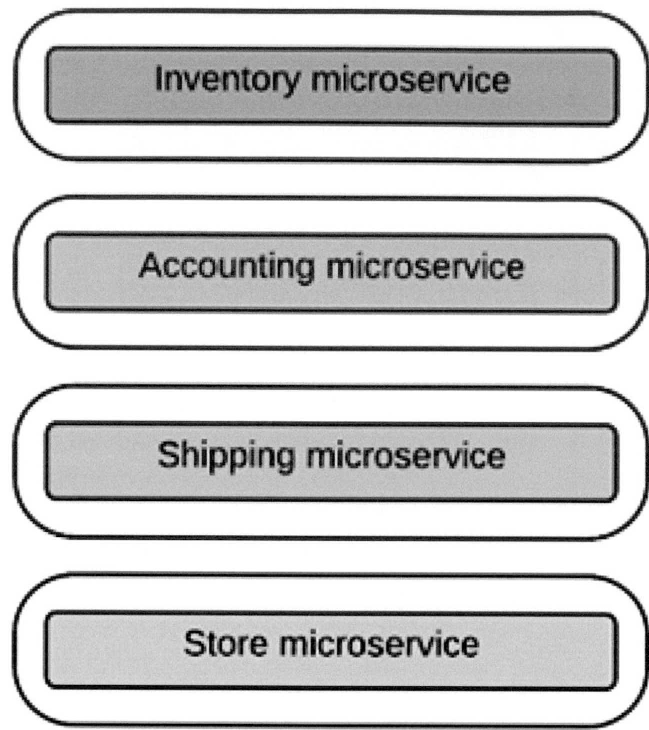


**Figure 3.2** Microservice architecture.

from the others. Instead, we should form smaller groups with all of the skills needed to build and manage the facilities they are responsible for. The position was defined by Amazon CTO Werner Vogel's as 'you develop it, you operate it'. There are several advantages to forming your teams in this manner [7].

First and foremost, your coders will get a better knowledge of how their code affects production – this will aid in the development of stronger releases and lower the likelihood of bugs being published to your consumers. Second, because your teams will be able to cooperate on code modifications and deployment pipeline automation, your releases will become second nature to them.

### 3.2.3 Create microservices architecture by splitting monolith architecture

You may start dividing your monolith into microservices once you have established the limits of your services and found out how to alter them in terms of competencies, your teams should be more vertical. Here are some essential considerations to make at that time (Figure 3.2).

Using a RESTful API, you can keep the lines of communication across services easy.

Now it is a wonderful opportunity to add a RESTful API into your company's architecture if you have not previously. You want complex endpoints and stupid processes, as one individual put it [8, 9]. This indicates that such communication protocol is in use for your service and are straightforward as possible with the only objective of conveying data without altering it. Everything will be handled by the endpoints, which will accept a query, process it, and deliver a result. Here is also how microservices are distinguished from SOA [10] by eliminating the Enterprise Service Bus's complexity. To prevent tight coupling of the components, microservice designs attempt to keep things as simple as possible. With asynchronous message-based interactions, you can find yourself employing an event-driven design in some situations. However, you should consider using basic message queuing services such as RabbitMQ to messages exchanged across the network should not be made more complicated (Figure 3.3).

#### 3.2.3.1 Divide the data structure into sections

In a monolith, it is customary to have a separate database for all of the varied functionalities. When a user views their order, the customer information is shown directly in the user database, and the same table may be used to build the billing system's invoice. This may appear reasonable and straightforward; however, with microservices, you will need to decouple the services so that bills may be accessed even if the purchasing system is down, and so that you can optimise or update the invoice table independently of others. As a result, each service may require its separate datastore to store the data it requires.

This obviously creates new issues because some data will be duplicated in multiple databases. In this case, this aims for eventual consistency and employs an event-driven architecture to help with data synchronization across several services [11, 12]. For example, when a client updates their personal information, your billing and delivery-tracking facilities may be listening for events broadcast by the account service. Those services will update their datastores as soon as the event is received. Because the account service logic does not need to know about all of the other dependent services, the event-driven design allows it to be kept simple. It just informs the system of what it has done, and other facilities listen and respond appropriately. You may also keep all customer information inside the account service and just preserve a foreign key reference in the invoicing and delivery function. Instead of duplicating existing records, they would interface with the account service to retrieve the necessary customer data as needed. There are no general answers

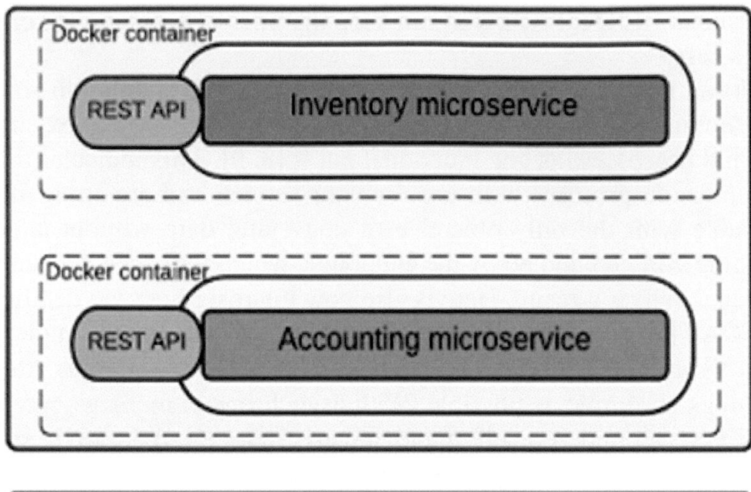


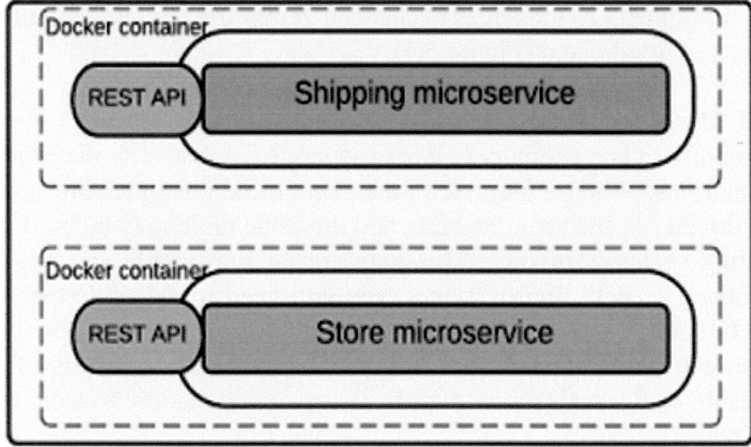


**Figure 3.3** Microservice architecture with REST API.

to these issues, so you will have to investigate each instance individually to identify the best course of action (Figure 3.4).

### 3.2.3.2 Make the microservices architecture fail-proof

We have viewed how microservices can be more cost-effective than monolithic designs. They are smaller and more specialised, making them easier to comprehend. They are separated, which implies you can redesign a service without causing other components to break off the system or hold down other teams' work. They also provide your developers greater freedom, since they may use various technologies as needed rather than being restricted by the requirements of other services [12, 13].

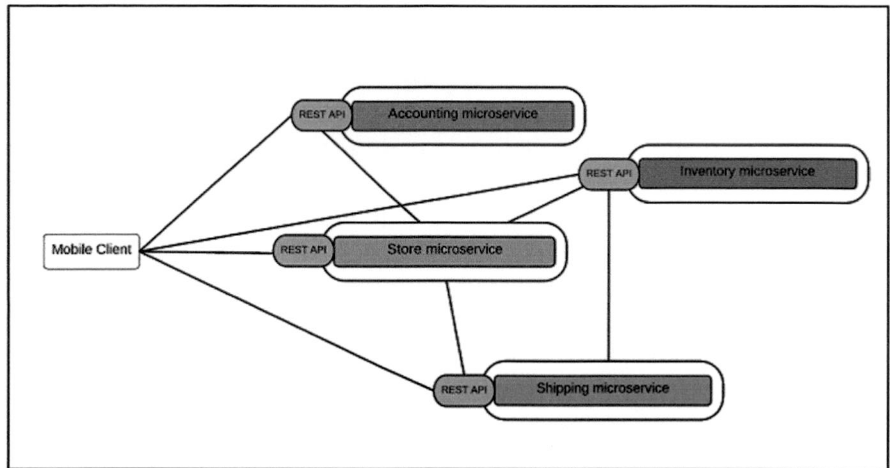


**Figure 3.4** Microservice architecture with inter-service communication.

In a summary, the microservice architecture simplifies the development and maintenance of each business feature. However, when all of the services are considered together, and they interact to perform activities, things get more difficult. You must account for the fact that your system is now dispersed and has several points of failure. You must be prepared to deal with not only the scenarios when a service is not responding but also delayed network replies. Recovering from the failure can be difficult at times because you must ensure that services that are restored, are not swamped with waiting messages. As you begin to remove capabilities from the monolithic systems, be sure that the designs are designed to fail from the start.

#### 3.2.3.3 To make microservices testing easier, emphasise monitoring

Microservices have another disadvantage as compared to monolithic systems: testing. To get a test environment up and going for the application that is created as a single codebase, you do not need much. To execute your test suite, you will almost certainly need to set up a backend server with a database. Things are not that simple in the realm of microservices. When it gets to unit testing, it will be fairly comparable to a monolith, and you should not have any extra difficulties [14]. However, things will become considerably more challenging when it relates to system integration and testing. You may need to start many services at the same time, have multiple datastores up and running, and include message queues in your configuration that you did not require with your monolith. Running functional tests becomes considerably more expensive in this environment, and the rising number of moving elements makes it impossible to foresee the many forms of errors that might occur. That is where you will need to place a strong focus on monitoring to detect problems early and respond appropriately. You will need to know the different service baselines and be ready to respond not only once they go offline but also while they behave strangely [15]. One benefit of using the microservice design is that your platform should be robust to breakdowns, so if you see irregularities in our Pizza Hub application's delivery tracking service, it will not be as terrible as it would be if it were a monolithic solution. While we restore live tracking, our software should be structured such that all the other services react smoothly, and our clients may buy pizzas.

#### 3.2.3.4 To eliminate deployment friction, embrace continuous delivery

Manually releasing the monolithic framework to production is a time-consuming and dangerous endeavour, but it is possible. Obviously, we do not support this strategy and strongly advocate each software team to adopt continuous delivery for all forms of development, but at the start of the project, you may want to conduct your own deployments through the command line. When we have a rising number of services that require to be delivered numerous times each day, this technique is no longer viable. As a result, embracing continuous delivery as part of your shift to microservices is crucial to reducing the risk of release failure and ensuring that the team is concentrated on creating and operating the application instead of trapped distributing it. Continuous delivery [16] also means that the service will have succeeded in the acceptance tests before being sent to production – defects will inevitably arise, but over time, you will construct the comprehensive test suite that will give the team more confidence in the quality of the releases (Figure 3.5).

Microservices are gradually gaining popularity as an industry best practice. They provide more versatility in the manner you may design and distribute software for complicated projects. They also aid in the identification and formalisation of your system's business components, which is useful when many teams are collaborating on the same project. However, there are certain evident disadvantages to maintaining distributed schemes, and dividing the monolithic design should just be done when the service boundaries are well understood. Microservices development should be viewed as a voyage rather than a short-term goal for a team [16]. Begin small to gain a better understanding of the technical needs of the distributed approach, as well as how to gracefully fail and grow the individual components. As you gain expertise and understanding, you may progressively extract more and more services.

The transition to a microservices architecture does not have to be completed all at once. A safer bet is to use an iterative technique to transition

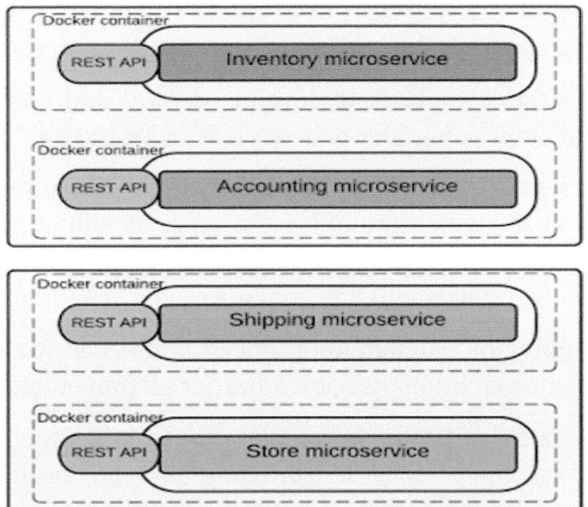


**Figure 3.5** Microservice architecture with deployment.

smaller components to microservices in stages. Identify the most well-defined service boundaries inside a monolithic application and decouple those into their individual microservice incrementally. To summarise, microservices is the model that benefits both the development of raw technical programming and the broader business approach. Microservices enable teams to be organised into units that are responsible for creating and owning certain business operations. This level of detail enhances overall corporate communication and efficiency. The advantages of microservices come at a cost. Before transitioning to a microservice design, service boundaries must be well specified. Although microservice architectures are still in their infancy, a promising method of designing applications is well worth investigating [17].

## 3.3 Principles of Microservices

- The microservice architectural style is an apprach to develop a single application as a suite of small services.
- It is a complex coalition of code, databases, application functions and programming logic spread across servers and platforms. Certain fundamental components of a microservices architecture bring all these substances together cohesively across a dispersed framework.
- It allows a large application to be separated into smaller independent parts, with each part having its own realm of responsibility. To serve a single client demand, a microservices-based application can call on

many internal microservices to compose its response. In the microservice architecture, all the services communicate with each other.

- It provides the framework to develop, deploy, and maintain microservices architecture diagrams and services independently.
- Containers are a appropriate microservices architecture example, since they let you focus on developing the services without worrying about the dependencies. Modern cloud-native applications are usually assembled as microservices utilising container.
- Supports polyglot programming. For example, services do not need to share the same technology stack, libraries or frameworks.

Microservices are utilised to accelerate application improvement. Microservices structures fabricated utilising Java are normal, particularly Spring Boot ones. It is additionally normal to analyse microservices versus administration-arranged engineering. Both have a similar goal, which is to separate solid applications into more modest parts, however, they have various methodologies.

Benefits of utilising an API passage include:

- It decouples clients from administrations. Administrations can be formed or refactored without expecting to refresh the clients in general.
- Administrations can utilise informing conventions that are not web agreeable, like AMQP [18].
- The API Gateway can perform other cross-cutting capacities like verification, logging, SSL end and burden adjusting.
- Out-of-the-container approaches, as for choking, storing, change or approval.

Each microservice has its own business layer and database. If we change one microservice, it does not affect the other services. These services communicate with each other by utilizing lightweight protocols such as HTTP or REST [18] or messaging protocols (Figure 3.6).

There are the following principles of microservices:

- Single responsibility principle
- Modelled around the business domain
- Isolated failure
- Culture of automation

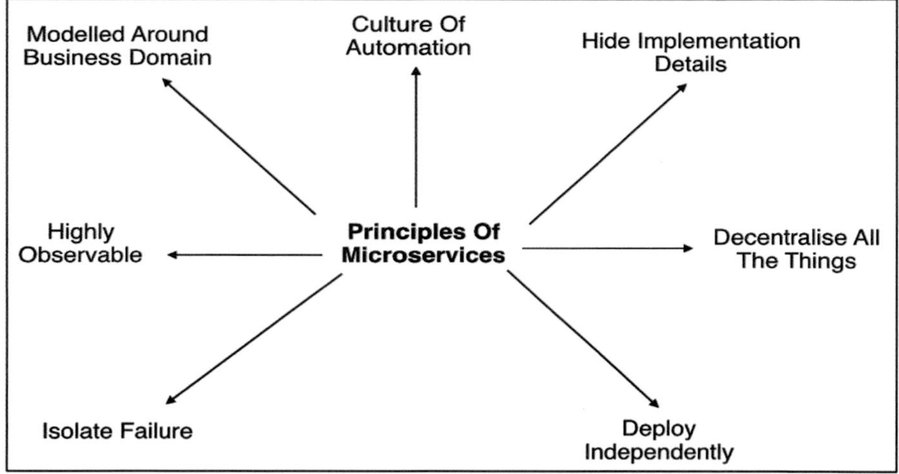


**Figure 3.6** Microservice principles.

- Deploy independently
- Highly observable
- Hide implementation details

### 3.3.1 Decentralisation

The single liability rule is one of the standards characterized as a feature of the SOLID plan design. It suggests that a unit, either a class, a capacity or a microservice, ought to have one and only one obligation. Never on schedule, one microservice ought to have more than one obligation [19].

### 3.3.2 Modelled around the business domain

Microservices should zero in on specific business works and guarantee that it helps in finishing things. A microservice will not ever confine itself from taking on proper innovation stack or backend information base capacity, which is generally appropriate for settling the business reason.

### 3.3.3 Isolated failure

A microservice-based structure is safer contrasted with solid construction. For instance, a failing microservice, for example, with a memory spill or unclosed data set associations, will just influence that help while different administrations keep on taking care of solicitations. In the event of a solid application, one failing part can cut down the whole framework.

### 3.3.4 Culture of automation

Getting ready and building a framework for microservices is another vital need. Assistance will be freely deployable and will package all conditions, including library conditions, and even execution conditions like web servers and compartments or virtual machines that are theoretical actual assets.

### 3.3.5 Deploy independently

To partake in the total advantages of the design, microservices ought to be autonomously deployable. Assuming you are neglecting to do as such, check for any coupling in the application and tackle it.

### 3.3.6 Highly observable

The administrations should gather as much data to examine what is going on inside every one of them like log occasions and details.

### 3.3.7 Hide implementation details

Microservices are little administrations with free lifecycles that cooperate as a piece of the entire application. Nevertheless, each help can be free when it must be a piece of the large design. To improve the capacity of one support of scale freely of the others, it is essential to conceal each help execution subtleties. We could utilise REST convention over HTTP and guarantee administrations speak with one another utilising a lightweight correspondence. Through this isolation of inward and outside execution, subtleties can be accomplished.

## 3.4 Major Consideration for Microservices Architecture

Microservice design is more perplexing than the inheritance framework. The microservice climate turns out to be more convoluted because the group needs to oversee and uphold many complex components. Here are portions of the top difficulties that an association face in its microservices venture:

- Bounded context
- Dynamic scale up and scale down
- Monitoring
- Fault tolerance
- Cyclic dependencies
- DevOps culture

### 3.4.1 Bounded context

The bounded context idea started in domain-driven design (DDD) circles. It advances the object model's first way to deal with administration, characterising an information model that help is answerable for and is bound to. A limited setting explains, typifies, and characterises the particular obligation to the model. It guarantees that the area would not be diverted from an external perspective. Each model should have a setting certainly characterised inside a sub-area, and each setting characterises limits.

### 3.4.2 Dynamic scale up and scale down

The heaps of the different microservices might be at an alternate occurrence of the sort. As well as auto-increasing your microservice should auto-downsize. It lessens the expense of the microservices. We can appropriate the heap progressively.

### 3.4.3 Monitoring

The conventional approach to observing would not adjust well to microservices since we have different administrations making up similar usefulness recently upheld by a solitary application. At the point when a blunder emerges in the application, observing the underlying driver can challenge.

### 3.4.4 Fault tolerance

Fault resilience is the singular assistance that does not cut down the general framework. The application can work at a specific level of fulfilment when disappointment happens. Without adaptation to internal failure, a solitary disappointment in the framework might cause a complete breakdown. The electrical switch can accomplish adaptation to internal failure. The electrical switch is an example that wraps the solicitation to outer help and distinguishes when they are broken. Microservices need to endure both inside and outer disappointment.

### 3.4.5 Cyclic dependency

Dependency on the executives across various administrations and its usefulness is vital. The cyclic reliance can make an issue, if not recognised and settled immediately.

### 3.4.6 DevOps culture

Microservices fits impeccably into DevOps. It gives quicker conveyance administration, deceivability across information, and financially savvy information. It can broaden their utilisation of containerisation change from service-oriented architecture (SOA) to microservice architecture (MSA).

## 3.5 Microservices Components

These are the main components:

- API
- Containers
- Service Mesh
- SOA
- Cloud

### 3.5.1 API

APIs and microservices are different yet reciprocal innovations. APIs work with coordination and correspondence between different administrations in microservices engineering, permitting administrations to ask for and get results from each other. This interoperability conveys the application's general usefulness.

### 3.5.2 Containers

Microservices are quite often connected with virtual holders, which are builds used to bundle administrations and their conditions. Holders can share a typical OS piece, which empowers them to exist on servers in far more noteworthy numbers. They likewise can be immediately turned up and destroyed, regularly in practically no time.

### 3.5.3 Service mesh

While APIs go about as the so-called stick for correspondence between administrations, the genuine rationale that oversees correspondence is another test. It is conceivable, but lumbering, to code correspondence rationale into each help in a normally intricate application.

All things being equal, microservices models regularly depend on a help lattice to digest administration to-support correspondence away from the administrations and into one more layer of the framework.

### 3.5.4 Software development approach (SDA)

SDA is a product improvement approach focused on joining reusable programming parts or administrations. A typical connection point permits the administrations to interoperate across a venture administration transport, yet requires little information on how each help functions. SDA parts frequently depend on XML and SOAP to convey. The SDA model turns out best for administrations that are generally conditional and reusable across huge programming frameworks.

### 3.5.5 Cloud

Containers and microservices can be conveyed and organised in any server farm or colocation office, yet they will require a framework that is intended to deal with such volumes of coordinated administrations, as well as fast or unusual scaling. Public mists give ideal conditions to on-request and adaptable registering, as well as coordination motors, API doors, pay-more only as costs arise authorising structures, and different components that go about as building blocks for microservices engineering.

## 3.6 Best Practices for Microservices

- Model administrations around the business area.
- Decentralise everything. Individual groups are liable for planning and building administrations. Try not to share code or information outlines.

- Information capacity should be private to the assistance that possesses the information. Utilise the best stockpiling for each assistance and information type.
- Administrations impart through all-around planned APIs. Try not to spill execution subtleties. APIs should demonstrate the space, not the inward execution of the help.
- Try not to couple between administrations. Reasons for coupling incorporate shared data set diagrams and inflexible correspondence conventions.
- Offload cross-cutting worries, like validation and SSL end, to the passage.
- Keep space information out of the passage. The door should deal with and course client demands with next to no information on the business rules or space rationale. In any case, the door turns into a reliance and can cause coupling between administrations.
- Administrations ought to have free coupling and highly useful attachment. Capacities that are probably going to change together ought to be bundled and sent together.
- Separate disappointments. Use versatility systems to keep disappointments inside assistance from falling. See Resiliency examples and Designing solid applications.

## 3.7 Core Benefits of Microservices

### 3.7.1 Agility

Since microservices are conveyed freely, it is simpler to oversee bug fixes and element discharges. You can refresh assistance without redeploying the whole application, and reign in an update if something turns out badly. In numerous conventional applications, on the off chance that a bug is found in one piece of the application, it can obstruct the whole delivery process. New elements might be held up sitting tight for a bug fix to be incorporated, tried and distributed.

### 3.7.2 Small but focused teams

A microservice should be little sufficient so that a solitary element group can assemble, test and convey it. Little group sizes advance more prominent readiness. Huge groups tend to be less useful, because correspondence is slower, the board upward goes up and deftness decreases.

### 3.7.3 Small code base

In a solid application, there is an inclination over the long haul for code conditions to become tangled. Adding another element requires contacting code in many spots. By not sharing code or information stores, a microservices design limits conditions, and that makes it simpler to add new highlights.

### 3.7.4 Mix of technologies

Groups can pick the innovation that best accommodates their administration, utilising a blend of innovation stacks as fitting.

### 3.7.5 Fault isolation

Assuming a singular microservice becomes inaccessible, it will not disturb the whole application, as long as any upstream microservices are intended to deal with deficiencies accurately [11].

### 3.7.6 Scalability

Administrations can be scaled freely, allowing you to scale out subsystems that require more assets, without scaling out the whole application. Utilising an orchestrator, for example, Kubernetes [20] or Service Fabric, you can pack a higher thickness of administrations onto a solitary host, which takes into account the more effective use of assets.

### 3.7.7 Data isolation

It is a lot simpler to perform mapping refreshes, because mainly a solitary microservice is impacted. In a solid application, blueprint updates can turn out to be exceptionally difficult, because various pieces of the application may all touch similar information, making any modifications to the mapping unsafe [12].

## 3.8 Conclusion

Since we are clear about what monolithic architecture is. Now it is time to switch back to another kind of architecture for developing applications that is using the microservice architecture. In the microservices architecture, the complete application is broken down into simpler and smaller services which are developed independently from each other. So, unlike a monolithic architecture where the complete application had the same database, here in microservices architecture each microservice will have its own database and its own technology stack. Microservices architecture has a lot of advantages but it also has its own set of disadvantages and complexity. The applications that are being developed using the monolithic architecture require a small team with some programming knowledge whereas, in a microservices architecture, one needs a bigger and more experienced team of developers who are well familiar with how microservice architecture works. Microservice architecture addresses many disadvantages of monolithic architecture, one of them being the issue of scaling. Unlike the monolithic architecture where you need to scale the application vertically only, here in microservices architecture as you can see in the diagram above you can scale the application horizontally as well as depending on the number of requests and traffic on a particular section of the application. In the above section of this chapter, we dive deep into the advantages and the disadvantages of using the microservices architecture, and finally, we concluded by comparing which one is better microservices architecture or monolithic architecture.

## References


[1] Lwakatare, L. E., Kuvaja, P. and Oivo, M. Relationship of DevOps to Agile, Lean and Continuous Deployment: A Multivocal Literature Review Study. Springer, City, 2016.

[2] Priyanka, T. K., Singh, M. K., & Kumar, A. (2022). Deep learning for satellite-based data analysis. Meta-heuristic Optimization Techniques: Applications in Engineering, 10, 173.

[3] Humble, J. and Molesky, J. Why enterprises must adopt devops to enable continuous delivery. Cutter IT Journal, 24, 8 (2011), 6.

[4] Pant, S., Kumar, A., Ram, M., Klochkov, Y., & Sharma, H. K. (2022). Consistency Indices in Analytic Hierarchy Process: A Review. Mathematics, 10(8), 1206.

[5] Kumar, A., Negi, G., Pant, S., Ram, M., & Dimri, S. C. (2021). Availability-Cost Optimization of Butter Oil Processing System by Using Nature Inspired Optimization Algorithms. Reliability: Theory & Applications, (SI 2 (64)), 188–200.

[6] Runeson, P. and Höst, M. Guidelines for conducting and reporting case study research in software engineering. Empirical software engineering, 14, 2 (2009), 131.

[7] H. K. Sharma, R. Tomar, A. Dumka and M. S. Aswal, "OpenECOCOMO: The algorithms and implementation of Extended Cost Constructive Model (E-COCOMO)," 2015 1st International Conference on Next Generation Computing Technologies (NGCT), 2015, pp. 773–778, doi: 10.1109/NGCT.2015.7375225.

[8] Sharma, Hitesh. "E-COCOMO: the extended cost constructive model for cleanroom software engineering." Database Systems Journal 4.4 (2013): 3–11.

[9] Sharma, Hitesh Kumar, et al. "Real time activity logger: a user activity detection system." Int J Eng Adv Technol 9.1 (2019): 1991–1994.

[10] Uniyal, N., Pant, S., Kumar, A., & Pant, P. (2022). Nature-inspired metaheuristic algorithms for optimization. Meta-heuristic Optimization Techniques: Applications in Engineering, 10, 1.

[11] Khanchi, Ishu, Ezaz Ahmed, and Hitesh Kumar Sharma. "Automated framework for real-time sentiment analysis." 5th International Conference on Next Generation Computing Technologies (NGCT-2019). 2020.

[12] Taneja, Sahil, et al. "AirBits: A Web Application Development using Microsoft Azure." ICRDSTHM-17) Kuala Lumpur, Malasyia (2017).

[13] H. K. Sharma, S. Kumar, S. Dubey and P. Gupta, "Auto-selection and management of dynamic SGA parameters in RDBMS," 2015 2nd International Conference on Computing for Sustainable Global Development (INDIACom), 2015, pp. 1763–1768.

[14] Sharma, H.K, Singh, S.K., Ahlawat, P. "Model-based testing: the new revolution in software testing." Database Syst J 4.1 (2014): 26–31.

[15] Sharma, Hitesh Kumar, et al. "SGA Dynamic Parameters: The Core Components of Automated Database Tuning." Database Systems Journal 5.2 (2014): 13–21.

[16] Sharma, Hitesh Kumar, et al. "An effective model of effort estimation for Cleanroom software development approach." ICRDSTHM-17) Kuala Lumpur, Malasyia (2017).

[17] Singh, Himmat, Aman Jatain, and Hitesh Kumar Sharma. "A review on search based software engineering." IJRIT Int. J. Res. Inform. Technol 2.4 (2014).

[18] Kumar, A., Pant, S., Ram, M., & Yadav, O. (Eds.). (2022). Meta-heuristic Optimization Techniques: Applications in Engineering (Vol. 10). Walter de Gruyter GmbH & Co KG.

[19] Sharma, Hitesh Kumar, et al. "Sensors based smart healthcare framework using internet of things (IoT)." International Journal of Scientific and Technology Research 9.2 (2020): 1228–1234.
[20] Dingsøyr, T. and Lassenius, C. Emerging themes in agile software development: Introduction to the special section on continuous value delivery. Information and Software Technology, 77 (2016), 56–60.

# 4

# Container: A Solution of Diverse Platform


## Abstract

Usage of diverse platform in the IT industry is a common culture. The different environments use different platforms for running the developed application. Running the same application in these different environments is a major challenge in IT industry. Containerisation is the only solution to overcome these challenges.

In this chapter, we have explained the working of containerisation. The advantage of using this culture is explained in this chapter in more detail.


## 4.1 Introduction

Virtual machines are well-known modular workable computing units. Containers are compared by virtual machines (VMs) to understand the core functionalities of containers. The container, however, is the product of a few OS-level virtualisation features of the Linux kernel. It is used to build a single lightweight environment. These are used to start the lightweight microservices. It is clear why containers are compared to VMs: they have their process trees, network, users, root and file systems. There is also a basic difference, between VMs and containers: containers use the kernel host and are responsible for launching the host OS only. These processes run individually or in groups on a hosted system, while VMs allow the installation of guest OS that may be different from the OS of the hosting system [1, 2].

IT engineers are very concerned about their applications. They should not ignore the importance of application space. The running application ensures application performance, functionality, and responsiveness to external factors. External factors include increased load and responsive app scaling accordingly. Such concerns are alleviated when IT developers ensure the appropriateness and flexibility of the application. It is also the responsibility of developers that the application can work in any environment without making changes to the source code of the application. Since each location may be different. Simply sending the source code for an app may not provide the expected flexibility [3].

The ideal solution would be to send the application code and dependency files packed into the box. The application should follow simple visual installation and uninstallation. These necessary requirements are fulfilled by container technologies. Containers provide isolation of developed applications with a running environment [4]. Based on technological advances today, customers expect faster development and faster deployment. Containers with microservices are a clear solution to customer needs because they increase the speed of development and raise the level of confidence in all shipments. Containers also allow the app and location to be recorded. Collaboration has been one of the key features of the containers. Having a few projects that use the same virtualisation features, each project deals with problems independently in its way, resulting in an even greater number of guidelines and rules. Users had to follow the stated requirements to use one container frame compared to another and they were not working together. Users of a particular type of container are locked in a specific workspace of a particular container. Over time, this became a problem that slowed down the overall development process. Gradually, well-defined sets of standards have been set to guide not only the construction process of the box images but also the configuration of the vessel's working space. Being able to move container images between different operating time zones, by allowing containers to interact and allowing them to be integrated with external company storage and network. Plugins for various projects and vendors are just a few of the benefits of container technology. For several years, the community has been divided between two different container standards – the App Container standard and the open container initiative [5]. After many years of competition between standards and their use in sequence, the community decided to establish a single integrated standard to regulate the performance of boxes in all arenas and operating times. To simplify the merging process between the two levels and avoid renaming the wheel, a few different features of the App Container level are designed to move slightly to Open Container Initiative. Image signing, dependency, and pod support are just a few of the features that are designed to be used in the Open Container Initiative. Although the integration process is relatively simple. The community can still make great strides in achieving a single integrated level of Open Container Initiative. As this new direction has been agreed upon, the App Container standard has not received any new features, with little support for its existing features. The

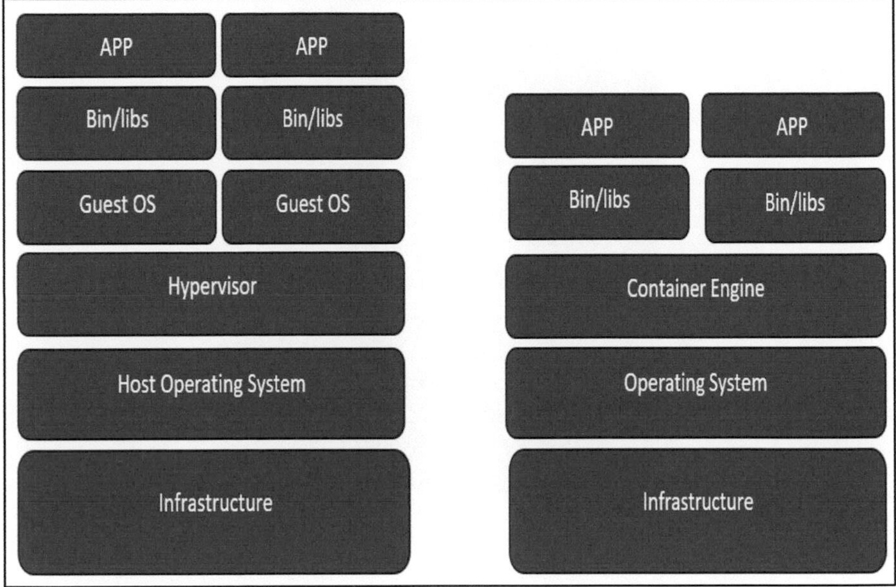


**Figure 4.1** Virtual machines and containers.

architectural difference between Virtual Machines and Containers is given in the following layered architecture (Figure 4.1).

## 4.2 Container as Microservice

Micro and Macro software organisations are appreciating microservices as an advanced technique for utility improvement. Compared to the previous monolithic version that integrates software with the related interface & underlying DB database right into an unmarried unit or an unmarried server platform. With microservices, a highly complex software application is fragmented into a sequence of tiny, more specialised offerings. Every with the DB database and commercial enterprise good judgment [6, 7]. With the usage of microservices, developer groups could recognition on upgrading specific regions of software without affecting the software application. The ideas or concepts for microservices and containerisation are comparable to the duo for software program improvement practices. Microservices and Containers are used to be useful for transportable, scalable, portable, efficient and simpler to manage. Furthermore, containerisation with microservices works great when used collectively. Containers ensure a lightweight easy encapsulation of software, whether the software service is a classical monolith

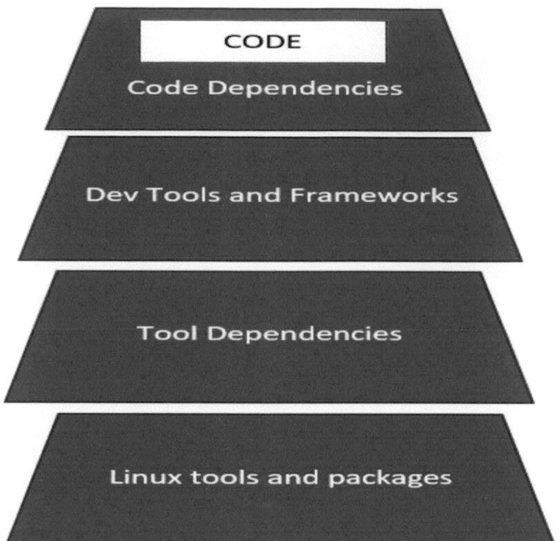


**Figure 4.2** Typical layers of a container image.

or a modular microservices [8]. A microservice with a container gains all the attached advantages of containerisation. It helps developers to speed up writing code, fault containment, server inefficiencies, automation of setup, upscaling, downscaling and management. These days communications (Telecommunications) are hastily shifting to the cloud wherein users can broaden programmes faster and correctly. Cloud-based software, applications and records are handy with any net-related smart device, permitting group individuals to paint remotely and on the cross.

Cloud carrier companies (CSPs) [9] control the abstracted infrastructure that saves companies money on servers and other systems. Additionally offers automatic community backups for extra reliability. Cloud infrastructures scale on demand and can dynamically alter computing resources, potential, and infrastructure as load necessities alternate. Containers, microservices and cloud computing are operating together to convey application development and shipping to new tiers not viable with traditional methodologies and environments. Those subsequent-era processes add agility, efficiency, reliability and protection to the software program development lifecycle. These results in quicker delivery of applications and upgrades to cease customers and the marketplace (Figure 4.2).

## 4.3 Container Storage

The complexity of Docker as a container management framework is also reflected in its ways to manage the storage of packaged applications. We will explore various storage concepts, access methods, storage drivers, and volume types as we learn how Docker handles storage and volumes in its containers. Unions are utilised by Docker to overlay a base container image with garage layers, consisting of an ephemeral storage layer, custom storage layer, and config. layer on the time a new container is created. The ephemeral storage is reserved for the boxes [7, 10] operations and it is not advocated for use for persistent records. Alternatively, a volume has to be set up on the field to provide continual storage no longer managed by UnionFS.

The replica-on-Write (Cow) strategy of UnionFS [11] lets users 'indirectly' modify the content material of documents available to the jogging field from the bottom field image storage layer. While the field image files are read-only. Instead, the bottom container picture document is copied and saved at the ephemeral garage layer of the box and the user is permitted to make modifications to the new reproduction of the record. In essence, a copy of a file is saved while a user tries to edit the examine-simplest file of the base field image. All the bottom box photo file remains intact. This method is used on the operating device level for reminiscence management and manner control. It is used by Docker to control the garage for container pix, and strolling boxes, and to reduce I/O and the dimensions of every storage layer.

## 4.4 Security

Packages have a degree of natural protection as they can serve as alternatives and may operate independently without other containers. When downloaded, this may protect you from any malicious code touching other drums or attacking the host machine. However, software layers within the field are usually shared across all bins. In terms of app efficiency, this includes, yet also opens the door for interruptions and security breaches in all boxes. The same can be said of a shared operating machine because a few barrels may be related to an active host machine.

Security threats on a normal operating system can affect all related boxes, and conversely, box violations may invade the host operating system. Box-era providers, along with Docker, continue to actively address the challenges of container protection. Containerisation has adopted a 'spontaneous' release process, which believes that security should be natural within the platform and not one response after another provided and modified [10, 12]. To this end, the container engine helps all the default isolation housings located within the active gadget. Protection permissions may be put in place to prevent robots from accessing packaging containers or limiting contact with unnecessary services.

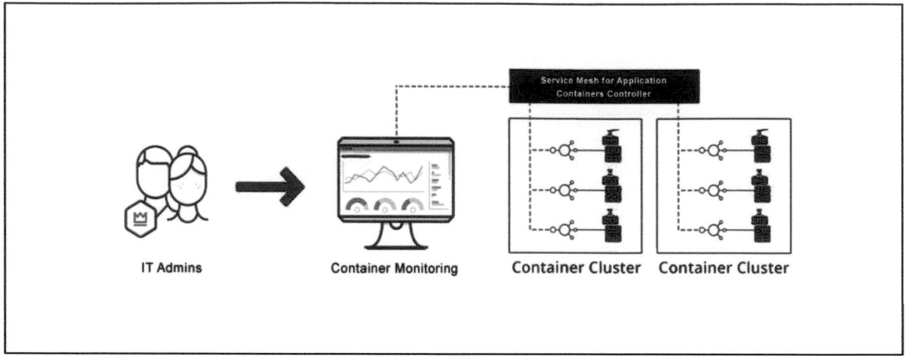


**Figure 4.3** Manual container monitoring process.

## 4.5 Container Monitoring

Container monitoring is the activity of ceaselessly collecting metrics and tracking the health of containerised applications and microservices conditions. It is used to work on their health and ensure their execution without any hindrances. Containers have become quite possibly the most famous method for conveying applications. For example, making it more straightforward for associations to further develop their application movability and functional versatility. In Cloud Native Computing Foundation (CNCF's) 2018 study [13, 14], 73% of respondents demonstrated they are right now involving compartments underway to support nimbleness and accelerate the pace of development. Compartment checking is a subset of discernibleness – a term regularly utilised next to each other with observing which likewise incorporates log conglomeration and investigation, following, warnings and perceptions. Contrasted with conventional observing arrangements, current checking arrangements give vigorous abilities to follow possible disappointments, as well as granular bits of knowledge into compartment conduct. This section covers the reason why, when, and how you should screen your holders, and what difficulties and arrangements you can pay special attention to (Figure 4.3).

The benefits of container monitoring include:

- Identify the issues that are proactive to avoid system outages.
- Monitoring time-series data, which will help applications, run better.
- Implement the changes safely by catching problems early and resolving the issues quickly.

Container monitoring solutions utilise metric catch, transaction tracing, analytics and visualisation. It covers fundamental metrics like memory use, CPU use, CPU limit and memory limit. It additionally offers the constant streaming logs, tracing and observability that containers need. This information can perceive an IT team when to scale up by providing use ratios. Application security monitoring can also be utilised.

Docker container performance checking and Kubernetes container monitoring require memory and CPU ratios for the actual cluster itself. If containers run an HTTP server, request counts and metrices connected with non-continuity must be collected. Comprehensive container monitoring considers the different layers in a stack and what each layer expects to work well. This incorporates text-based error information, for example, 'could not connect with data set' or 'container restart'. Both numeric and text-based information is significant for container monitoring to track.

### 4.5.1 Options for container monitoring

To accelerate development cycles and build governance into their CICD (continuous integration and continuous development) pipeline. Teams can build responsive tooling and scripts into their standard DevOps orchestration by utilising metrices from their monitoring solution or leveraging local area projects. Autopilot is a monitor-and-react engine. It watches the measurements from the applications that it is monitoring and based on specific circumstances being met in those metrics. It responds and alters the application's runtime environment. It is the best illustration of a project designed to make it easier for businesses to make metric-based decisions. Businesses that have put resources into Chaos Engineering will need to isolate and profile failure areas to enhance their risk resilience tooling [15]. Chaos Monkey, initially made by Netflix, randomly terminates virtual machine instances and containers that run within the production environment. This exposes engineers to failures much more frequently. By infusing failures into a failure however not having a good set of metrics by which to track them you are really just left with chaos.

For containerised applications running on AWS assets, a similar cross-information source monitoring experience can be acknowledged with Amazon Cloud Watch Container Insights. Via naturally gathering and putting away measurements and logs from arrangements like FluentD and DockerStats, CloudWatch Container Insights can give you knowledge about your compartment groups and running applications [14][16].

## 4.6 Conclusion

In this chapter, we have discussed that a container is a standard software unit that packs code and all its dependencies so that the application can run quickly and reliably from one computer location to another. Docker Container Image is a lightweight, standalone, user-friendly software package that covers everything needed to run an app: code, operating time, system tools, system libraries and settings. Container images become containers during operation and in the case of Docker containers – Images become containers when working in the Docker engine. Available on both Linux and Windows-based applications, the container-based software will always work the same way, regardless of infrastructure. Containers separate the software in its place and ensure that it works the same despite the differences for example between upgrades and the platform.

## References

[1] Uniyal, N., Pant, S., Kumar, A., & Pant, P. (2022). Nature-inspired metaheuristic algorithms for optimization. Meta-heuristic Optimization Techniques: Applications in Engineering, 10, 1.

[2] Ståhl, D. and Bosch, J. Modeling continuous integration practice differences in industry software development. Journal of Systems and Software, 87 (2014), 48–59. Hitesh Kumar Sharma; Anuj Kumar; Sangeeta Pant; Mangey Ram, "6 Application of Blockchain in Smart Healthcare," in Artificial Intelligence, Blockchain and IoT for Smart Healthcare , River Publishers, 2022, pp. 57–66.

[3] Priyanka, T. K., Singh, M. K., & Kumar, A. (2022). Deep learning for satellite-based data analysis. Meta-heuristic Optimization Techniques: Applications in Engineering, 10, 173.

[4] Pant, S., Kumar, A., Ram, M., Klochkov, Y., & Sharma, H. K. (2022). Consistency Indices in Analytic Hierarchy Process: A Review. Mathematics, 10(8), 1206.

[5] Kumar, A., Negi, G., Pant, S., Ram, M., & Dimri, S. C. (2021). Availability-Cost Optimization of Butter Oil Processing System by Using Nature Inspired Optimization Algorithms. Reliability: Theory & Applications, (SI 2 (64)), 188–200.

[6] Sharma, Hitesh KUMAR. "E-COCOMO: the extended cost constructive model for cleanroom software engineering." Database Systems Journal 4.4 (2013): 3–11.

[7] Sharma, Hitesh Kumar, et al. "Real time activity logger: a user activity detection system." Int J Eng Adv Technol 9.1 (2019): 1991–1994.

[8] Khanchi, Ishu, Ezaz Ahmed, and Hitesh Kumar Sharma. "Automated framework for real-time sentiment analysis." 5th International Conference on Next Generation Computing Technologies (NGCT-2019). 2020.

[9] Taneja, Sahil, et al. "AirBits: A Web Application Development using Microsoft Azure." ICRDSTHM-17) Kuala Lumpur, Malasyia (2017).

[10] H. K. Sharma, S. Kumar, S. Dubey and P. Gupta, "Auto-selection and management of dynamic SGA parameters in RDBMS," 2015 2nd International Conference on Computing for Sustainable Global Development (INDIACom), 2015, pp. 1763–1768.

[11] Sharma, Hitesh KUMAR, Sanjeev KUMAR Singh, and Prashant Ahlawat. "Model-based testing: the new revolution in software testing." Database Syst J 4.1 (2014): 26–31.

[12] Sharma, Hitesh Kumar, et al. "SGA Dynamic Parameters: The Core Components of Automated Database Tuning." Database Systems Journal 5.2 (2014): 13–21.

[13] Sharma, Hitesh Kumar, et al. "An effective model of effort estimation for Cleanroom software development approach." ICRDSTHM-17) Kuala Lumpur, Malasyia (2017).

[14] Kumar, A., Pant, S., Ram, M., & Yadav, O. (Eds.). (2022). Meta-heuristic Optimization Techniques: Applications in Engineering (Vol. 10). Walter de Gruyter GmbH & Co KG.

[15] Sharma, Hitesh Kumar, et al. "I-Doctor: An IoT based self patient's health monitoring system." 2019 International Conference on Innovative Sustainable Computational Technologies (CISCT). IEEE, 2019.

[16] Lwakatare, L. E., Kuvaja, P. and Oivo, M. Relationship of DevOps to Agile, Lean and Continuous Deployment: A Multivocal Literature Review Study. Springer, City, 2016.

# 5

# Container Monitoring: A Container Health Check Process

## Abstract

In containerisation, an application needs to run multiple containers simultaneously. For each microservices there needs to be one or more containers associated. Monitoring the health of these containers is not manually possible. There are many open-source and proprietary tools for doing this process automatically. In this chapter, we have presented some majorly used tools for container monitoring. We have also presented the dashboards of all picked-up tools.

## 5.1 Introduction

Container monitoring is the activity for continuously collecting metrics and continuously checking the health of containerised applications. Container monitoring is used to work on their health and ensure their execution without any hindrance. Containers became quite possibly the most famous method for launching an application. The main focus of using a container is making it more straightforward for associations amongst the IT teams. In cloud native computing foundation (CNCF's) 2018 study, 73% of respondents demonstrated [1] that they have enhanced their development and deployment process after integrating containers into their framework. Container monitoring is another main activity after integrating containers into their framework. Generating logs, collecting logs, and timely processing them are the main challenges in container monitoring. Contrasted with conventional observing arrangements, current checking arrangements are more feasible. This chapter covers the reason why, when and how you should screen your holders, and what difficulties and arrangements you can pay special attention to (Figure 5.1).

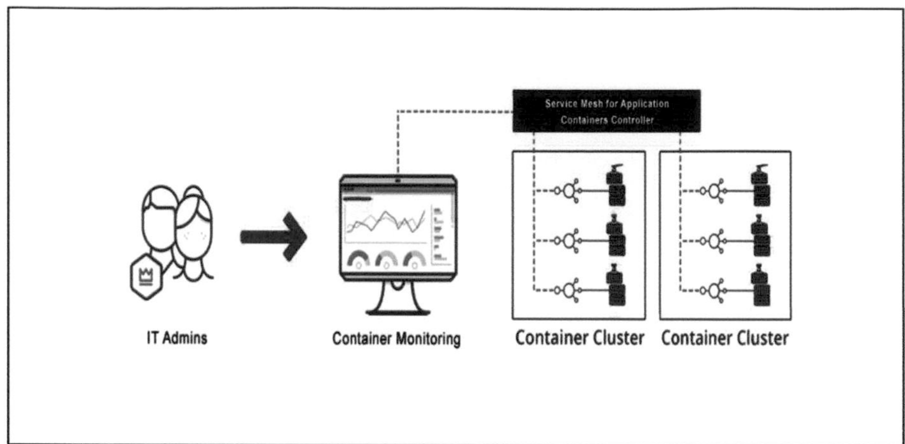


**Figure 5.1** Container monitoring process.

Container monitoring solutions utilise metric catch, transaction tracing, analytics and visualisation. It covers fundamental metrics like memory use, CPU use, CPU limit and memory limit. It additionally offers the constant streaming logs, tracing and observability that containers need [2] (Figure 5.1).

This information can perceive an IT team when to scale up by providing use ratios. Application security monitoring can also be utilised. Docker container performance checking and Kubernetes container monitoring require memory and CPU ratios for the actual cluster itself. If containers run an HTTP server [3], request counts and metrices connected with non-continuity must be collected.

Comprehensive container monitoring considers the different layers in a stack. It also considers what each layer expects to work well. The text-based information helps to monitor the container performance. Some textual parameters are analysed to check the health of the container against the threshold value [4, 5].

## 5.2 Container Monitoring

To accelerate development cycles and build governance into their CICD (continuous integration and continuous development) pipelines, teams can build responsive tooling and scripts into their standard DevOps orchestration. AutoPilot from Portworx provides some solutions for utilising metrices. Autopilot is a monitor-and-react engine [6]. It watches the measurements from the applications. Based on its monitoring and based on specific circumstances being met in those metrices, it responds and alters the application's runtime environment. It is used to build to control stateful applications deployed on Kubernetes. It is the best illustration of a project designed to make it easier for businesses to make metric-based decisions.

Businesses that have put resources into Chaos Engineering will need to isolate and profile failure areas to enhance their risk resilience [7, 8]. Chaos Monkey, initially made by Netflix, randomly terminates virtual machine instances and containers that run within the production environment. This exposes engineers to failures more frequently. By infusing failures into a failure however not having a good set of metrics by which to track them you are really just left with chaos [9].

For containerised applications running on Amazon Web Service assets, a similar cross-information source monitoring experience can be acknowledged with Amazon Cloud Watch Container Insights [10, 11]. Via naturally gathering and putting away measurements and logs from arrangements like FluentD and DockerStats, CloudWatch Container Insights can give you knowledge about your compartment groups and running applications.

### 5.2.1 Monitoring Docker container

Docker container performance monitoring includes the following:

- Detecting the problems early.
- Tracking entire environments when making changes and upgrades.
- Refining applications for better performance (Figure 5.2).

## 5.3 Container Monitoring Tools

Monitoring containers is not the same as checking conventional arrangements as in the two cases you wanted measurements, logs, administration revelation and well-being checks. It is more intricate because of its dynamic and complex nature. However, a decent compartment-checking arrangement can explore every one of the layers inside a stack.

The most useful tools for container monitoring are as follows.

### 5.3.1 Sematext

Sematext monitoring is a full-stack recognisability arrangement with Docker checking capacities. It gives a far-reaching, simple-to-set-up, observing dashboard for measurements, occasions and logs, giving you significant

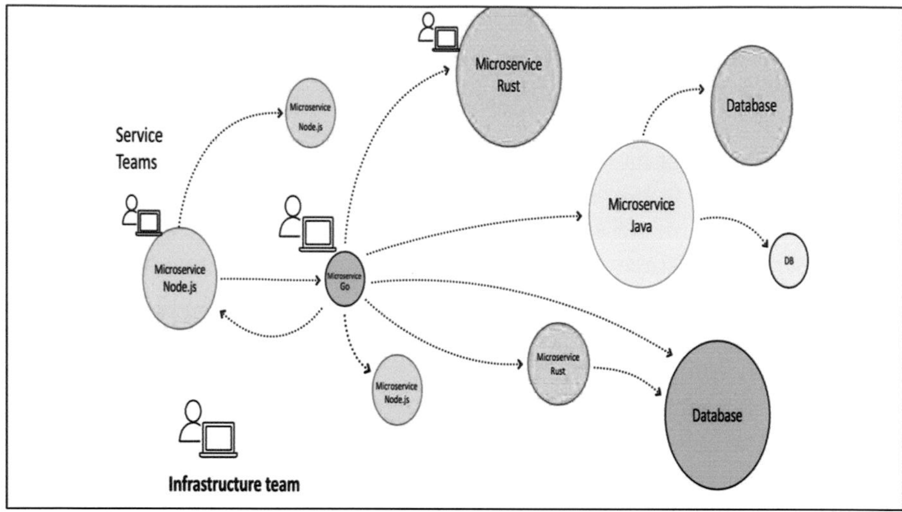


**Figure 5.2** Process flow diagram for container monitoring.

experiences about holders and foundations. With abnormality location, cautioning and relationships between all pieces of your foundation, bunches and compartments, you get all that you really want in one spot, for better and quicker investigating (Figure 5.3).

Sematext auto-revelation naturally recognises new compartments and containerised applications running in them and allows you to begin administrations and log checking and benefits straightforwardly through the UI without additional means (Figure 5.4).

## 5.3.2 Datadog

Datadog gives a powerful checking framework to your foundation, applications, organisation and logs, while additionally offering support for Docker compartments. Everything necessary is introducing the Datadog specialist. On the off chance that you now have the specialist introduced, you are all set. On the off chance that you do not, simply download the specialist bundle and adhere to the directions. The main thing to remember is that 350 measurements for every checked example are performed. You can likewise naturally assemble Docker logs to have full perceivability in your compartments (Figure 5.4).

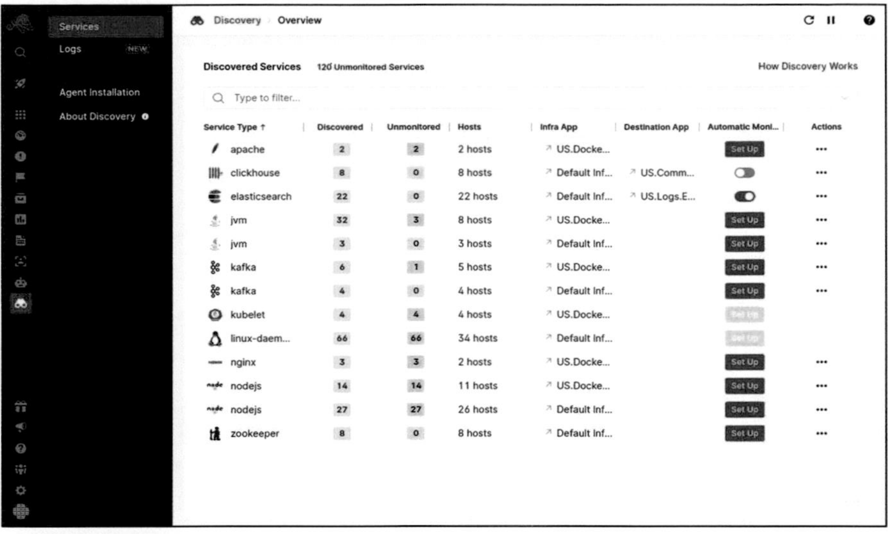


**Figure 5.3** Sematext monitoring tool dashboard.

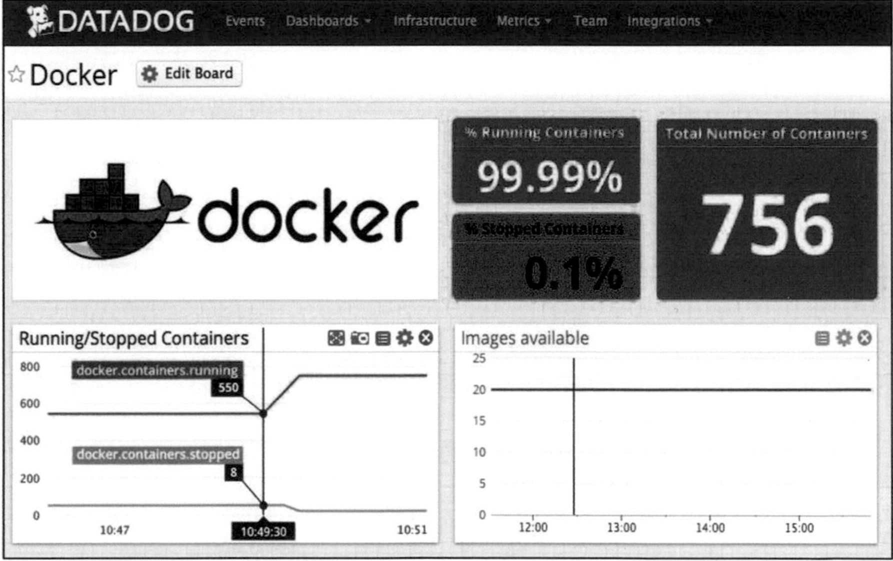


**Figure 5.4** Datadog monitoring tool dashboard.

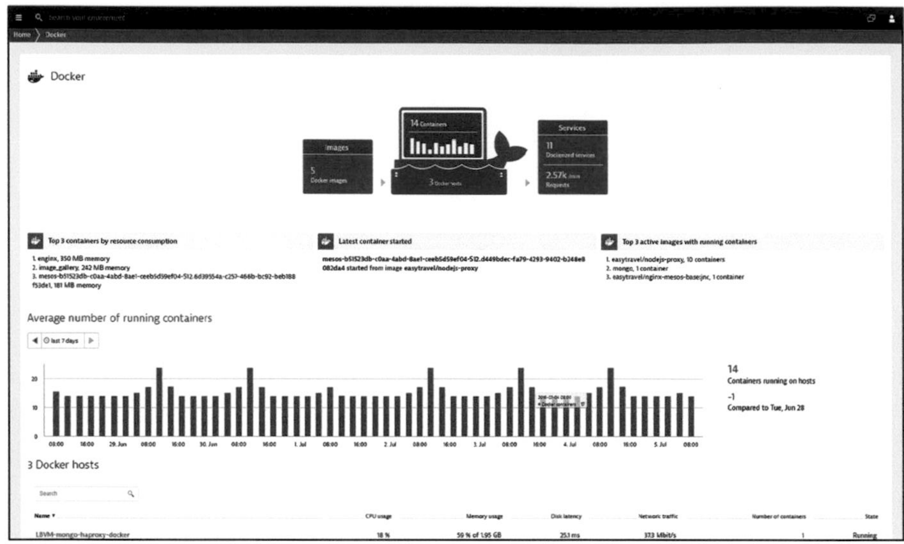


**Figure 5.5** Dynatrace monitoring tool dashboard.

### 5.3.3 Dynatrace

Dynatrace is additionally a full-stack discernibleness arrangement that gives an easy-to-understand way to deal with observing your Docker holder measurements and logs. Accessible in both programming as assistance (SaaS) and on-premise models it will satisfy the vast majority of your checking needs. Dynatrace allows you to investigate holder asset utilisation of particular hosts. Similarly, you can collect execution details for further action. You can collect core information of Docker measurements like CPU utilisation, RSS and store memory use, both approaching and active organisation traffic (Figure 5.5).

### 5.3.4 Elasticsearch and Kibana

Elasticsearch is a web search tool given the Lucene library. It gives a circulated, multitenant competent full-text web crawler with an HTTP web connection point and blueprint-free JSON reports. Elasticsearch is created in Java. Elasticsearch allows you to store, search and investigate easily at scale.

Kibana is a free and open UI that allows you to imagine your Elasticsearch information and explore the elastic stack. Do anything from following the inquiry burden to understanding how solicitations move through your applications. Kibana center boats with works of art: histograms, line diagrams, pie outlines, sunbursts, from there, the sky is the limit. Furthermore, you can

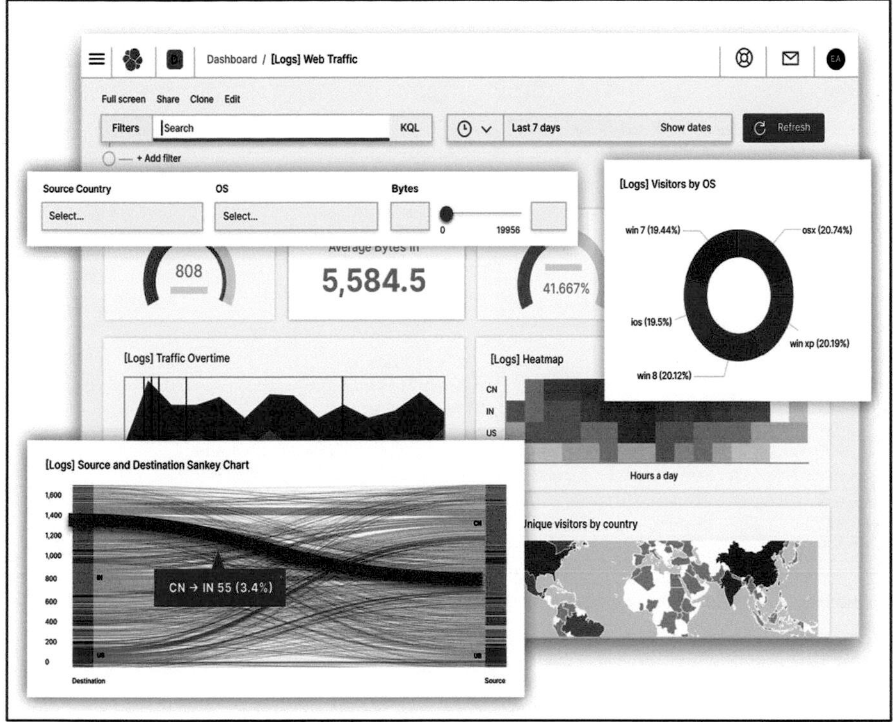


**Figure 5.6** Elastic and kibana monitoring tool dashboard.

look across your archives in general. Another strong open-source combo is Elasticsearch and Kibana joins incredible adaptability with a backend giving checking to Docker compartment logs. Nonetheless, very much like with Prometheus and Grafana, the underlying arrangement and design step as well as continuous redesigns, support and so on will be required and might be tedious and subsequently exorbitant, particularly if you are curious about the apparatuses (Figure 5.6).

### 5.3.5 SolarWinds server and application monitor

SolarWinds server and application monitor give observing to Docker compartments. It gives you an understanding of Docker measurements close by Windows and Linux measurements relying upon your preferred climate. With cautioning upheld out-of-the-case and dashboarding abilities the arrangement is a decent contender for observing Docker as well as your whole framework (Figure 5.7).

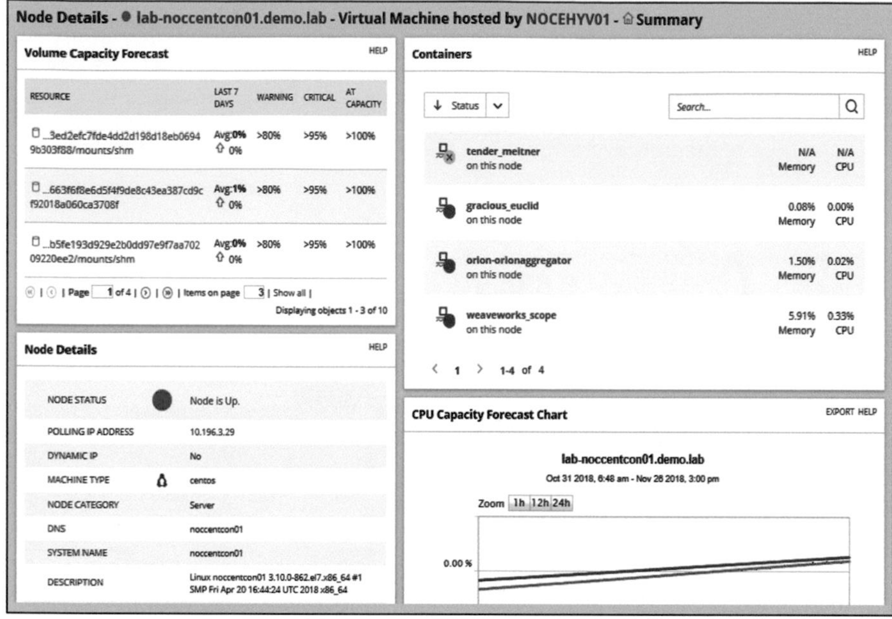


Figure 5.7 SolarWinds server monitoring tool dashboard.

### 5.3.6 AppOptics Docker monitoring with APM

AppOptics is a full-stack APM that empowers you to assess application execution and allows you to consider your containerised assets to be well. With AppOptics you can recognise execution issues rapidly and distinguish whether they are being brought about by the compartments or the code running in them. AppOptics is presently important for Solarwinds. The elements you get from SolarWinds Server and Application Monitor and AppOptics are comparable (Figure 5.8).

You get an out-of-the-case docker joining with effective use measurements, including CPU usage, to give the presentation bits of knowledge you want. You can likewise design cautions to send consequently when your docker measurements surpass set edges.

## 5.4 Conclusion

In cloud native computing foundation's (CNCF) 2018 study, 73% of respondents demonstrated they are right now involving compartments underway to support nimbleness and accelerate the pace of development. Compartment checking is a subset of discernibleness a term regularly utilised next to each

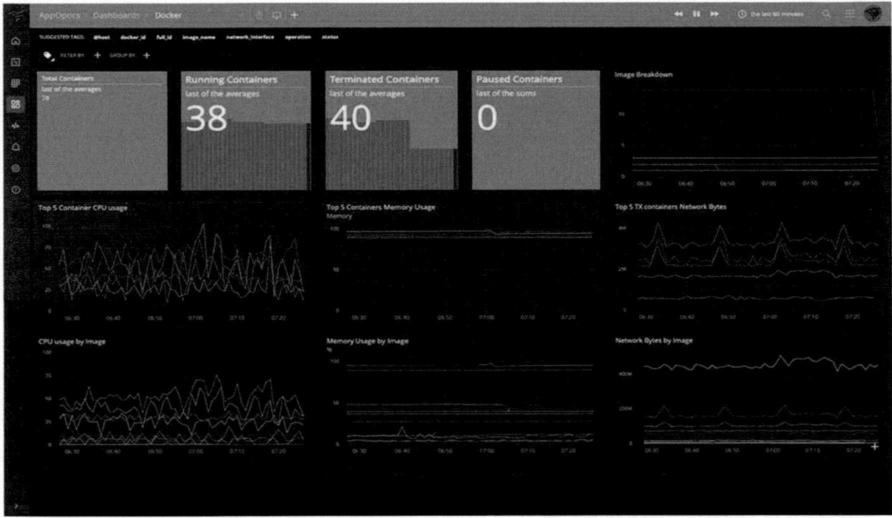


**Figure 5.8** AppOptics monitoring tool dashboard.

other with observing which likewise incorporates log conglomeration and investigation, following, warnings and perceptions. Contrasted with conventional observing arrangements, current checking arrangements give vigorous abilities to follow possible disappointments, as well as granular bits of knowledge into compartment conduct. This chapter covers the reason why, when and how you should screen your holders, and what difficulties and arrangements you can pay special attention to. Container monitoring is the activity of ceaselessly collecting metrics and tracking the health of containerised applications and microservices conditions, to work on their health and ensure their execution without any hindrance. Containers have become quite possibly the most famous method for conveying applications, bringing advantages, for example, making it more straightforward for associations to further develop their application movability and functional versatility.

## References

[1] Clear, T. THINKING ISSUES: Meeting employers expectations of devops roles: can dispositions be taught? ACM Inroads, 8, 2 (2017), 19–21.

[2] Eck, A., Uebernickel, F. and Brenner, W. Fit for continuous integration: How organizations assimilate an agile practice (2014).

[3] Ståhl, D. and Bosch, J. Modeling continuous integration practice differences in industry software development. Journal of Systems and Software, 87 (2014), 48–59. Hitesh Kumar Sharma; Anuj Kumar; Sangeeta Pant; Mangey Ram, "6 Application of Blockchain in Smart Healthcare," in Artificial Intelligence, Blockchain and IoT for Smart Healthcare , River Publishers, 2022, pp.57–66.

[4] Hitesh Kumar Sharma; Anuj Kumar; Sangeeta Pant; Mangey Ram, "7 Security and Privacy challenge in Smart Healthcare and Telemedicine systems," in Artificial Intelligence, Blockchain and IoT for Smart Healthcare , River Publishers, 2022, pp.67–76.

[5] Sharma, H. K., Khanchi, I., Agarwal, N., Seth, P., & Ahlawat, P. (2019). Real time activity logger: A user activity detection system. Int J Eng Adv Technol, 9(1), 1991–994.

[6] Jabbari, R., bin Ali, N., Petersen, K. and Tanveer, B. What is DevOps?: A Systematic Mapping Study on Definitions and Practices. XP2016, ACM, 2016. [14] Walls, M. Building a DevOps Culture. O'Reily Medis, Inc., 2013.

[7] Sharma, H. K., Kumar, S., Dubey, S., & Gupta, P. (2015, March). Auto-selection and management of dynamic SGA parameters in RDBMS. In 2015 2nd International Conference on Computing for Sustainable Global Development (INDIACom) (pp. 1763–1768). IEEE.

[8] Sharma, H. K., Singh, S. K., & Ahlawat, P. (2014). Model-based testing: the new revolution in software testing. Database Syst J, 4(1), 26–31.

[9] Sharma, H. K., Jindal, M., Munjal, K., & Jain, A. (2017). An effective model of effort estimation for Cleanroom software development approach. ICRDSTHM-17) Kuala Lumpur, Malasyia.

[10] Kumar, A., Pant, S., Ram, M., & Yadav, O. (Eds.). (2022). Meta-heuristic Optimization Techniques: Applications in Engineering (Vol. 10). Walter de Gruyter GmbH & Co KG.

[11] Lwakatare, L. E., Kuvaja, P. and Oivo, M. Relationship of DevOps to Agile, Lean and Continuous Deployment: A Multivocal Literature Review Study. Springer, City, 2016.

# 6

# Docker: An Open-Source Containerisation Platform


## Abstract

Creating and managing containers required a well-managed platform and open-source tool. Docker is the most famous and useful tool for containerization. Google Kubernetes is also using Docker as a base for creating containers. Docker-Hub is a public registry to store Docker images. In this chapter, we have explained the architecture of Docker and some basic commands for handling Docker.


## 6.1 Introduction

Docker is a free and open-source containerisation platform. It enables programmers to bundle their applications into containers. Containers are standardised executable components that integrate application source code with the Operating system libraries. It ensures running that code in any specific circumstance. It is built on the concept of packaging your code and dependencies into a deployable unit known as a container. Docker ensures that all developers have access to all the components of the product they are working on [1]. As a result, if someone adds software dependencies, they will be available to everyone when they are needed. There is no need for this if there is only one developer. A container is an independent programming bundle that contains everything expected to run an application, including code, runtime, framework instruments and framework libraries.

## 6.2 Docker: A Containerisation Platform

### 6.2.1 Working of Docker

- Docker embodies an application alongside each of the conditions in a virtual container that can be sent off on any Linux framework. To this end, they are alluded to as containers since they contain each of the expected conditions in a solitary piece of programming.

- A daemon that forms, runs and deals with the containers. It is a significant level API that permits the client to speak with the Docker engine and a CLI that makes it all suitable [2].

### 6.2.2 Purpose of Docker

- We should look at some specific use cases of Docker containers.
- Docker is used when the same application needs to run on multiple different platforms. Only the Docker engine is required to run the Docker container on any platform.
- Docker provides microservices for almost all applications.
- Docker volume and Docker network provide the facility to communicate multiple containers together.

### 6.2.3 Benefits of Docker

- Docker helps to run multiple microservices together.
- It is useful for effectively sharing resources.
- Scalability: a single host can accommodate many containers.
- Using far less expensive hardware than traditional servers to run your service.
- Fast deployment, easy creation of new instances and migrations are all advantages.
- Moving and managing your applications is simple.
- Better security, fewer software dependencies and less access to the code operating inside containers.

## 6.3 Significance of Docker

Organisations use Docker as an option in contrast to virtual machines for multiple reasons. Docker is used as a substitute since it utilises fewer assets than virtual machines. Virtual machines are intended to mimic virtual equipment though containers share working frameworks. Docker applications can run with a small amount of the assets of a virtual machine since they share working frameworks. As opposed to the virtual asset escalated PCs used by virtual machines, Docker utilises the Docker engine, which is facilitated on a solitary Linux occurrence. Due to this construction, Docker containers might uphold over multiple times the quantity of server application cases that a virtual machine would be able. Docker's inescapable notoriety has likewise been worked with by the way that engineers might tweak and send lean applications by adding their code. These applications can then be introduced straightforwardly on machines or in the cloud.

### 6.3.1 Performance

As you can see, Docker has certain built-in advantages, thanks to its structure. Virtual machines cannot share a kernel or application libraries, but containers can. Additionally, Docker consumes fewer PC assets than virtual machines. Docker is less asset escalated progressively and can fire up altogether quicker than virtual machines. The justification behind this is that virtual machines should stack a working framework with every startup. Also, like virtual machines, containers do not need asset distribution [3, 4].

### 6.3.2 Portability

Those wishing to maximise networking resources should consider the portability of each technology. Docker containers are independent applications that suddenly spike in demand for their own. Docker containers are easy to port since they do not have separate working frameworks. They can fire up surprisingly fast whenever they have been ported, making them the more compact choice. Virtual machines, then again, are less compact since they each have their working framework. This makes them badly designed because the working framework cannot be effectively moved to another stage. Docker is better in situations where you want to send a scope of projects to settle various difficulties. The detachment of the working framework from the working arrangement of the host gadget guarantees that the applications can work without interference.

### 6.3.3 Security

The main point of contention between VM support and Docker is which arrangement is safer [5, 6]. This is a particularly difficult topic to tackle because there are so many variables to consider, from Docker's inherent weaknesses to the hypervisor's single point of failure.

## 6.4 Container Operations

The container is a process that works on a hosting system. This process is triggered by the operating time of the container from the container image, and the operating time provides a set of container process management tools. The container is a remote place that includes an active application and operates based on the configuration defined in the container image. During operation, virtualisation features found at the kernel level are attached to the container process to help manage various aspects of the physical environment of the container. Word spaces make the PID of the container process easier, network, root, and users [7]. Collections help to set restrictions on the use of the application in the host process that we can use in the host system, and security content uses the container process permissions we have in the host system. Container, as a timeline, uses common resources or any operating system that can consume the system: file system storage and any stored filesystems, CPU, memory, and connections to provide traffic to/from external clients, and other containers, or in-device devices [8, 9].

List running containers.

```
$ docker container ls
```

Running a container, -t option assigns pseudo-TTY, and -I option keeps STDIN open in interaction mode.

```
$ docker container run -it --name myalpine alpine sh
```

Attach a running container.

```
$ docker container attach myalpine
```

Run a container in the background with the –d option, in which case we receive an output with the container ID

```
$ docker container run -d alpine sh
```

Display container logs:

```
$ docker container logs <container ID>
```

Stop a running container:

```
$ docker container stop <container ID>
```

Start a stopped container:

```
$ docker container start <container ID>
```

Deleting or removing a container

```
$ docker container stop <container ID>
```

```
$ docker container rm <container ID>
```

Display all the details of a container

```
$ docker container inspect
```

```
$ docker container inspect <container ID>
```

## 6.5 Docker installation

Docker can be installed on Windows, Linux, Mac, and Ubuntu.

### 6.5.1 Docker installation on windows

To install Docker on windows, the system should meet all the requirements:

- Windows 11 64-digit: form 21H2 or higher for Home or Pro, or adaptation 21H2 or higher for Enterprise or Education.
- Home or Pro.
- On Windows, WSL 2 feature (enabled). Refer to the Microsoft manual for more information.

You will need the following hardware:

- Second Level Address Translation on a 64-bit CPU (SLAT)
- 4 GB RAM for the system
- Hardware virtualisation support at the BIOS level.
- Install the Linux kernel update package after downloading it.

#### 6.5.1.1 Installation steps

Download the Docker installer, and you can secure the installer (Docker Desktop Installer.exe) from Docker Hub on the off chance that you have not beforehand. It, as a rule, downloads to your Downloads organiser; yet, you may likewise execute it from the lower part of your internet browser's new downloads bar.

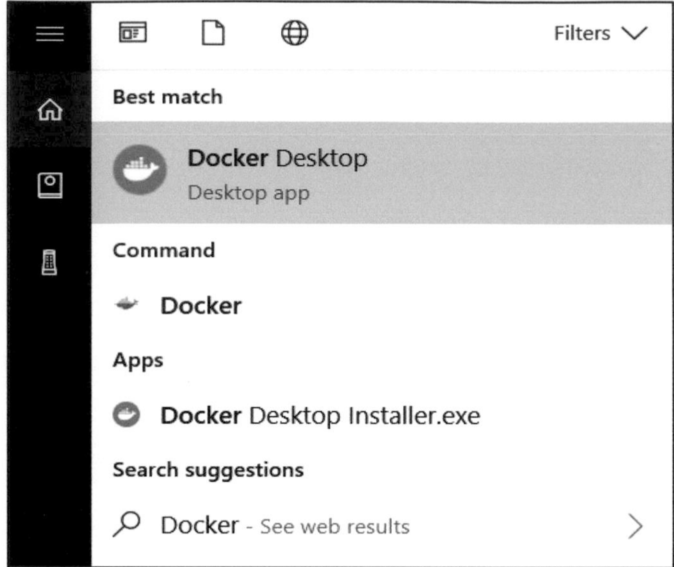


**Figure 6.1** Docker Desktop in windows OS program list.

#### 6.5.1.2 Starting Docker

After establishment, Docker Desktop does not begin consequently. To make Docker Desktop ready, follow these means.

- In the search results, type in Docker and pick Docker Desktop (Figure 6.1).
- Here you can click on the Docker Desktop icon and after that, quick start guide will start.

#### 6.5.1.3 Quick start guide

- Docker Desktop dispatches the Quick Start Guide after the beginning up is finished. This course incorporates a straightforward activity that includes making a Docker picture, running it as a compartment, and afterwards pushing and saving the picture to Docker Hub.
- To run the Quick Start Guide on request, enter the Docker Desktop menu by right-tapping the Docker symbol in the Notifications region (or System plate) and choose Quick Start Guide (Figure 6.2).

Congratulations! Docker Desktop is now running successfully.

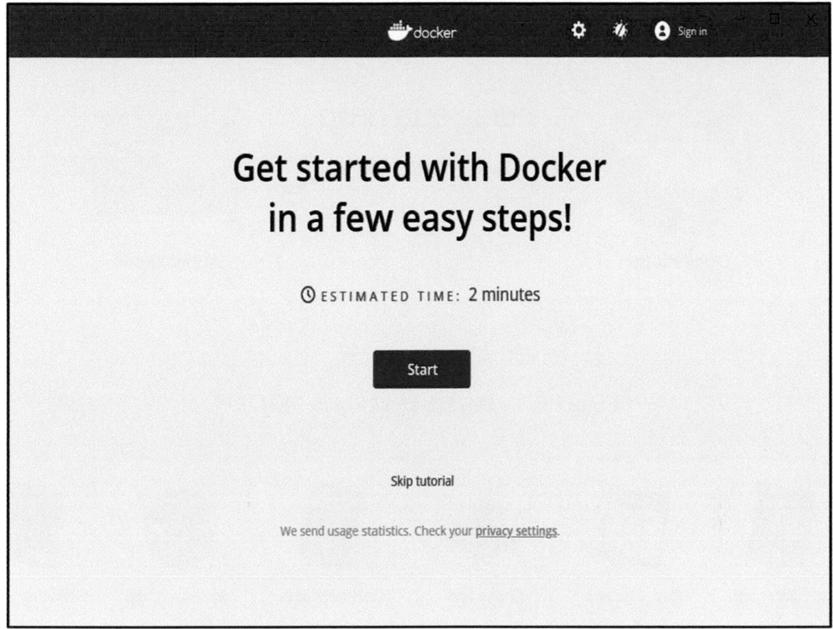


**Figure 6.2** Docker Desktop installation wizard.

#### 6.5.1.4 Uninstall Docker

- To uninstall Docker Desktop from your Windows PC, follow these means: Select Docker Desktop from the rundown of Apps and Features, then Uninstall. To affirm your decision, click Uninstall.

### 6.5.2 Installation on Mac

#### 6.5.2.1 System requirements

To install Docker Desktop successfully, your Mac must match the following criteria.

- MacOS 10.15 or later is required. Catalina, Big Sur, or Monterey, to be exact. We prescribe that you update to the latest rendition of macOS (Figure 6.3).
- On the off chance that you have any issues in the wake of moving up to macOS 10.15, you should refresh Docker Desktop to the latest variant to be viable with this form of macOS.
- 4 GB of RAM.

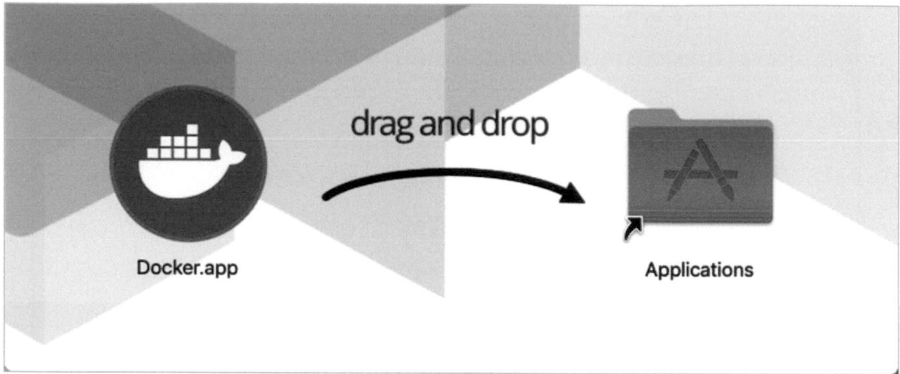


**Figure 6.3** Docker Desktop in MAC OS.

**Figure 6.4** Docker Desktop App in MAC OS program list.

- Virtual Box versions before 4.3.30 must be avoided since they are incompatible with Docker Desktop.

  Install and run Docker on Mac:

- To open the installer, double-click Docker.dmg.
- To start Docker, click on Docker; folder is shown in "grid" view mode in the example below (Figure 6.4).

### 6.5.2.2 Quick start guide

Docker Desktop runs the Quick Start Guide on the off chance that you have quite recently introduced the application. A basic activity to develop a model Docker image, run it as a container, then, at that point, push and save the picture to Docker Hub is remembered for the instructional exercise (Figure 6.5).

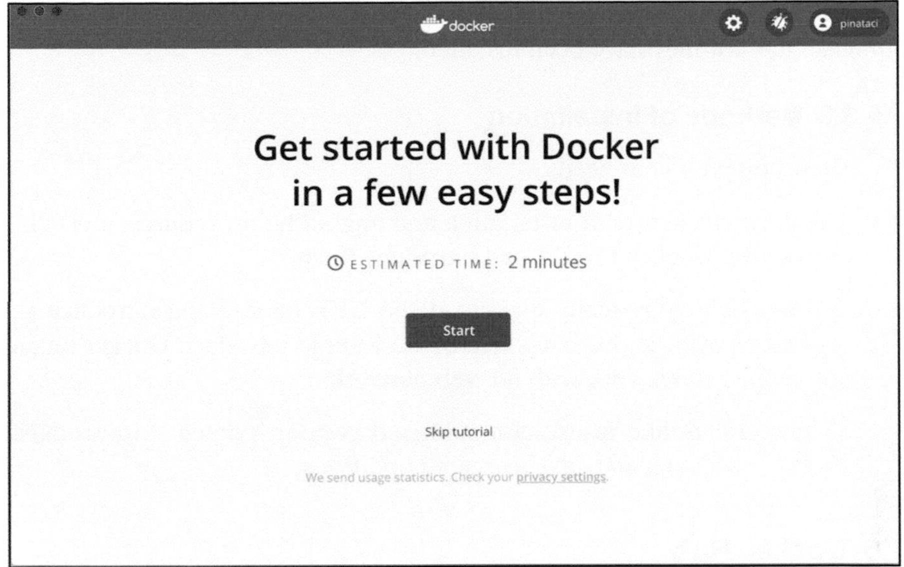


**Figure 6.5** Docker Desktop quick start guide wizard.

Congrats! Docker Desktop is as of now effectively running. To get to Preferences and different choices, go to the Docker menu (whale menu). Select the Docker menu and afterwards Quick Start Guide to send off the Quick Start Guide on request.

#### 6.5.2.3 Updates

Docker Desktop shows a symbol on the Docker menu when an update is free to connote the accessibility of a more up-to-date form. Furthermore, the Software Updates part of Preferences (Settings on Windows) will advise you of any Docker Desktop refreshes that are accessible. You may either download the overhaul immediately or read the Release Notes to study what is happening in the new form.

Clients on all Docker memberships, including Docker Personal and Docker Pro, have the choice to switch off the programmed check for refreshes beginning with Docker Desktop 4.2.0. See Software Updates for additional subtleties.

### 6.5.3 Docker installation on Ubuntu

#### 6.5.3.1 OS requirements

- Ubuntu 20
- Ubuntu 18

#### 6.5.3.2 Remove any previous versions

Uninstall these if they have been installed.

#### 6.5.3.3 Methods of installation

- Depending on your needs:
- For the convenience of installation and upgrading procedures, most clients set up Docker's vaults and introduce them.
- A few clients physically download the DEB bundle and introduce it, as well as oversee overhauls. Here you want to introduce Docker on an air-gapped framework with no web network.
- A few clients like to use computerised comfort content to introduce Docker in testing and advancement conditions.

## 6.6 Docker Hub

Docker Hub is a registry service for Docker Inc.'s repository. It allows us to upload and download Docker images from and to Docker Hub [10]. We can think of it like GitHub, where we download and push our source code, but with Docker Hub, we download and publish our container images. It is an online cloud-based repository that stores both public and private repositories. Everyone has access to public repositories, but only the repository owner has access to private repositories; there is also a cost connected with private repositories if we keep more than a specific number of repositories.

### 6.6.1 Features of the Docker Hub

The following are some of the features that Docker Hub has to offer.

#### 6.6.1.1 Repository of images

- It allows us to search for and download container images from Docker Hub.
- It also assists us in uploading images to the Docker Hub as a public or private repository.

#### 6.6.1.2 Organisations and teams

- It enables us to build workgroups and push repositories as private repositories that are only accessible within our organisation.

- We were able to control access to our private container image repositories in this way.

#### 6.6.1.3 Integration with GitHub and Bit Bucket

- It supports GitHub and Bit Bucket as well as other source code repositories.

#### 6.6.1.4 Automated builds

- It identifies and generates container images from GitHub or Bitbucket and pushes them to Docker Hub if any changes in the source code have been submitted to source code repositories.

#### 6.6.1.5 Webhooks

- Once we have successfully pushed our images, a webhook is used to perform an operation that integrates Docker Hub with other services [11, 12].

## 6.7 AWS Fargate

AWS Fargate is an answer that permits you to run containers on Amazon ECS without overseeing servers or groups of Amazon EC2 occurrences [9]. Fargate dispenses with the necessity for virtual machine bunches to be provisioned, designed, or scaled to run compartments. This disposes of the need to choose server sorts, plan group scaling, or enhance bunch pressing. Within a cluster, a task is the instantiation of a task definition. You can define the number of tasks to run on your cluster once you establish a task definition for your application in Amazon ECS. You can run a task as part of a service or as a standalone process. A logical grouping of jobs or services is an Amazon ECS cluster. Clusters can be used to isolate applications [13].

## 6.8 Docker Lifecycle

### 6.8.1 Development

This is the stage where you develop your code, make changes, and commit to the Version Control System, which you usually do in the development phase using the Continuous Integration philosophy (Figure 6.6).

### 6.8.2 Build code and Dockerising application

In this section, we will create a code and create its artefact, later we will integrate the application within the Docker image from Dockerfile [11].

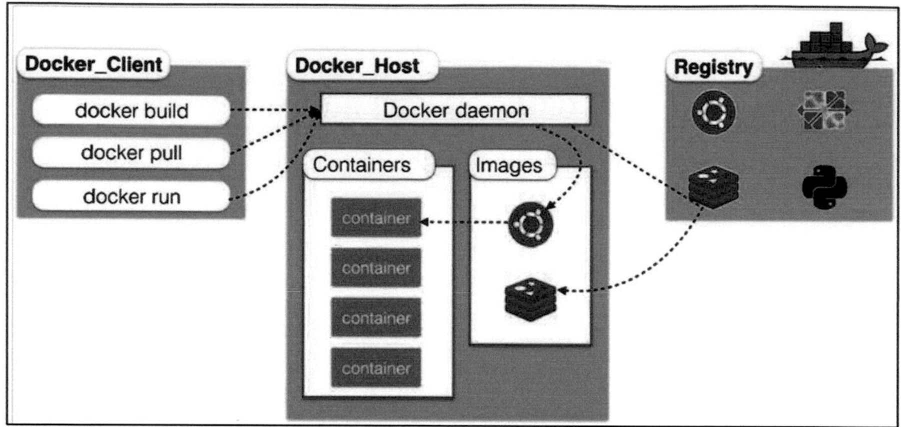


**Figure 6.6** Docker architecture.

### 6.8.3 Pushing the Docker image into a private registry

Once we have created a port image, we will check the code locally and push it into the private dock registration area to send it to advanced locations.

### 6.8.4 Deploying it into the testing environment

Now, we have a Docker image in your private dock registration, drag the latest dock image to the appropriate location and use that image in the test area to apply test conditions and other test features.

### 6.8.5 Host

Once we are satisfied that everything is working properly in the previous locations, we can live using the latest dock image.

## 6.9 Conclusion

Docker is one of the most popular containerisation tools. It is an open-source tool. We have seen the different components of the Docker platform. It is a free and open-source containerisation platform. It enables programmers to bundle their applications into containers, which are standardised executable components that integrate application source code with the Operating system libraries and conditions, which are expected to run that code in any specific circumstance. It is built on the concept of packaging your code and dependencies into a deployable unit known as a container. Docker ensures that all developers have access to all of the components of the product they are working on. As a result, if someone adds software dependencies, they will be available to everyone when they are needed. There is no need for this if there is only one developer. It is an independent programming bundle that contains everything expected to run an application, including code, runtime, framework instruments, framework libraries, and settings.

## References

[1] Debois, P. Devops: a software revolution in the making? Cutter IT Journal, 24, 8 (2011).

[2] Hitesh Kumar Sharma; Anuj Kumar; Sangeeta Pant; Mangey Ram, "2 Advanced Technologies Involved in Smart Healthcare and Telemedicine Systems," in Artificial Intelligence, Blockchain and IoT for Smart Healthcare , River Publishers, 2022, pp.13–24.

[3] Riungu-Kalliosaari, L., Mäkinen, S., Lwakatare, L. E., Tiihonen, J. and Männistö, T. DevOps Adoption Benefits and Challenges in Practice: A Case Study. Springer, Cham, 2016, 590–597.

[4] Hitesh Kumar Sharma; Anuj Kumar; Sangeeta Pant; Mangey Ram, "3 Role of Artificial Intelligence, IoT and Blockchain in Smart Healthcare," in Artificial Intelligence, Blockchain and IoT for Smart Healthcare , River Publishers, 2022, pp.25–36.

[5] Dyck, A., Penners, R. and Lichter, H. Towards definitions for release engineering and DevOps. In Proceedings of the Proceedings of the Third International Workshop on Release Engineering (Florence, Italy, 2015). IEEE Press.

[6] Pant, S., Kumar, A., Ram, M., Klochkov, Y., & Sharma, H. K. (2022). Consistency Indices in Analytic Hierarchy Process: A Review. Mathematics, 10(8), 1206.

[7] Sharma, H. K., Khanchi, I., Agarwal, N., Seth, P., & Ahlawat, P. (2019). Real time activity logger: A user activity detection system. *Int J Eng Adv Technol*, *9*(1), 1991–1994..

[8] Khanchi, I., Ahmed, E., & Sharma, H. K. (2020, March). Automated framework for real-time sentiment analysis. In *5th International Conference on Next Generation Computing Technologies (NGCT-2019).*

[9] Sharma, H. K., Kumar, S., Dubey, S., & Gupta, P. (2015, March). Auto-selection and management of dynamic SGA parameters in RDBMS. In *2015 2nd International Conference on Computing for Sustainable Global Development (INDIACom)* (pp. 1763–1768). IEEE.

[10] Sharma, H. K., Singh, S. K., & Ahlawat, P. (2014). Model-based testing: the new revolution in software testing. *Database Syst J*, *4*(1), 26–31. Sharma, Hitesh Kumar, et al. "SGA Dynamic Parameters: The Core Components of Automated Database Tuning." Database Systems Journal 5.2 (2014): 13-21.

[11] Sharma, H. K., Jindal, M., Munjal, K., & Jain, A. (2017). An effective model of effort estimation for Cleanroom software development approach. *ICRDSTHM-17) Kuala Lumpur, Malasyia.*

[12] Kumar, A., Pant, S., Ram, M., & Yadav, O. (Eds.). (2022). Meta-heuristic Optimization Techniques: Applications in Engineering (Vol. 10). Walter de Gruyter GmbH & Co KG.

[13] Singh, H., Jatain, A., & Sharma, H. K. (2014). A review on search based software engineering. *IJRIT Int. J. Res. Inform. Technol*, *2*(4).

# 7

# Docker Container: Volume and Network


## Abstract

Docker containers have many components in their ecosystems. Docker volume and Docker network are two main components. Docker volume is used for persisting the data inside a container and the Docker network is used for connecting the different containers to make them communicable with each other. Using a Docker volume, containers can also share the data. In this chapter, we have explained the significance of Docker volume and Docker network and the commands related to these components.


## 7.1 Introduction

Docker is an open-source containerisation tool which is Linux-based.

Unlike virtual machines, Docker compartments offer:

- Operating system level deliberation with ideal asset use
- Interoperability
- Effective form and test
- Quicker application execution

On a very basic level, Docker compartments modularise an application's usefulness into various parts that permit sending, testing and scaling them autonomously. For example, a Docker is a data set of an application. With such a structure, you can also scale or keep up the data set autonomously from the different modules or the parts of the application without affecting the jobs of the other basic frameworks [1].

## 7.2 Docker Architecture

### 7.2.1 Parts of Docker

Docker has different components within its core architecture, which comprises:

- Images
- Containers
- Registries
- Docker Engine

#### 7.2.1.1 Images

Images are the outlines, having the guidelines and the information for making the Docker holder.

Images characterise:

- Application conditions.
- When the application dispatches the cycle should run.

You can get all the images from Docker Hub [2] or make your own images by containing explicit guidelines inside the record called Dockerfile [3].

#### 7.2.1.2 Containers

Containers are live occurrences in images on which the application and its free modules are running. In an article situated programming relationship, an image is a class and the holder is an example of that class which permits functional productivity and permits numerous holders from a solitary image.

#### 7.2.1.3 Registries

A Docker registry resembles the storehouse of images. The default registry is the Docker Hub, a public vault storing public and official images for various dialects or stages. Naturally, solicitation of images from a Docker is looked at inside the Docker Hub vault [4]. Likewise, you can possess a private vault and arrange it as the default wellspring of images for your custom necessities.

#### 7.2.1.4 Docker Engines

The Docker Engine is the middle piece of a Docker framework on which the application is running. Also, you can, even in like manner, consider the

Docker Engine as the application that is presented with a structure that regulates holders, images and containers.

A Docker Engine utilises a client-server design and comprises the accompanying sub-parts:

- **The Docker Daemon** is fundamentally the server that suddenly spikes in demand for the host machine. It is liable for building and overseeing Docker images.
- **The Docker Client** is an order line interface (CLI) for sending guidelines to the Docker Daemon utilising exceptional Docker orders. However, a client can run on the host machine, it depends on Docker Engine's REST API [5] to associate from a distance with the daemon.
- **A REST API** upholds associations between the client and the daemon.

## 7.3 Docker in Software Development Life Cycle

Docker has various advantages that empower the application design. Docker brings some advantages to various phases of the software development lifecycle (SDLC) [6].

### 7.3.1 Build

It permits advancement to groups that save time, exertion and also cash by Dockerising the applications in a single module.

### 7.3.2 Testing

In Docker, you autonomously test each containerised application and its parts without affecting different parts of the application. Likewise empowers a structure by overlooking firmly coupled conditions and empowering unrivalled adaptation to non-critical failure.

### 7.3.3 Deploy and maintain

Docker lessens the grinding between groups by guaranteeing predictable renditions of libraries and bundles are utilised at each phase of the advancement cycle. In addition, conveying an all-around tried holder kills the presentation of bugs into the form interaction, in this manner empowering an effective movement to creation.

## 7.4 Managing Data in Docker

In Docker, data by default is stored in a writable container layer. This means that the data does not endure when that compartment does not exist anymore, and it tends to be challenging to get the information out of the holder assuming another interaction needs it. A holder's writable layer is firmly coupled to the host machine where the compartment is running. You can only with significant effort move the information elsewhere. Composing into a holder's writable layer requires a capacity driver to deal with the filesystem. The capacity driver gives an association filesystem, utilising the Linux bit. This additional reflection decreases execution when contrasted with utilising information volumes, which compose straightforwardly to the host filesystem.

## 7.5 Docker Volumes

Volumes are the favoured instrument for continuing information produced by and utilised by Docker compartments. While tie mounts are reliant upon the catalogue construction and OS of the host machine, volumes are totally overseen by Docker. Volumes enjoy a few upper hands over tie mounts:

- Volumes are more straightforward to back up or move than tie mounts.
- You can oversee volumes utilising Docker CLI orders or the Docker API.
- Volumes work on both Linux and Windows holders.
- Volumes can be more securely divided between various holders.
- Volume drivers let you store volumes on remote cloud suppliers, encode the substance of volumes, or add other usefulness.
- New volumes can have their substance pre-populated by a compartment.
- Volumes on Docker Desktop have a lot better exhibition than tie mounts from Mac and Windows.

Likewise, volumes are frequently a preferred decision over persevering information in a compartment's writable layer.

### 7.5.1 Use cases for volumes

Volumes are the favoured method for enduring information in Docker holders and administrations. Some utilisation cases for volumes include:

- Dividing information between various running compartments. On the off chance that you do not unequivocally make it, a volume is made whenever it first is mounted into a compartment. Whenever that holder stops or is eliminated, the volume actually exists. Numerous compartments can mount a similar volume at the same time, either read-compose or peruse as it were. Volumes are possibly taken out when you unequivocally eliminate them.
- Whenever the Docker is not ensured to have a given catalogue or document structure. Volumes assist you with decoupling the setup of the Docker from the holder runtime.
- Whenever you need to store your holder's information on a remote host or a cloud supplier, rather than locally.
- Whenever you really want to back up, re-establish, or move information starting with one Docker have then onto the next, volumes are a superior decision. You can stop holders utilising the volume, then, at that point, back up the volume's catalogue (e.g., /var/lib/docker/volumes/<volume-name>).
- Whenever your application requires superior execution I/O on Docker Desktop. Volumes are put away in the Linux VM rather than the host, and that implies that the peruses and composes have a lot lower inactivity and higher throughput.
- At the point when your application requires a completely local document framework conducted on Docker Desktop. For instance, an information base motor requires exact command over circle flushing to ensure exchange sturdiness. Volumes are put away in the Linux VM and can make these certifications, though tie mounts are remoted to macOS or Windows, where the record frameworks act somewhat in an unexpected way.

Docker volume is a generally utilised and helpful device to guarantee information determination while chipping away at holders. Docker volumes document frameworks are introduced in Docker holders to store information created by the dynamic compartment.

Docker has two compartment choices for putting away records on the host machine so that documents endure even after holder arrangement. Volumes are put away in the host document part, overseen by Tie mounts can be put away in any place in the facilitating framework. The information does not deal with when the compartment is as of now not accessible, and it very well might be hard to separate information from the holder assuming another interaction requires it. The removable compartment layer is immovably appended to the host machine where the holder works. The information would not be quickly moved somewhere else. Composing on a removable compartment layer requires a capacity driver to deal with the document framework. Volumes are a favoured strategy for constant information created and utilised by Docker holders. While tie mounts depend on the record design and OS of the host machine, the volumes are completely constrained by Docker [8].

**Volumes enjoy a couple of upper hands over tie mounts:**

- Volumes are more straightforward to reinforce or relocate than to tie.
- You can oversee volumes utilising the Docker CLI orders or the Docker API.
- Volumes work on both Linux and Windows holders.
- Volumes can be securely divided among various compartments.
- Volume drivers permit you to save volumes for remote hash or cloud suppliers, encode volume content, or add other usefulness.
- New volumes can have their substance pre-filled by the compartment.
- Volumes in Docker Desktop have a lot better presentation than mounting boilers from Mac and Windows.

### 7.5.2 Utilisations of volumes

- Decoupling holder from capacity
- Share Volume(Storage/information) among various Containers
- Joined volume to the holder
- On erasing holder volume does not erase

### 7.5.3 Docker volume commands

- Docker volume: Used to get information (Figure 7.1).
- Docker volume create: used to create a volume (Figure 7.2).
- Docker volume ls: to list the volumes (Figure 7.3).
- Docker volume inspect <volume_name>: used to get the details about the volume we have created (Figure 7.4).

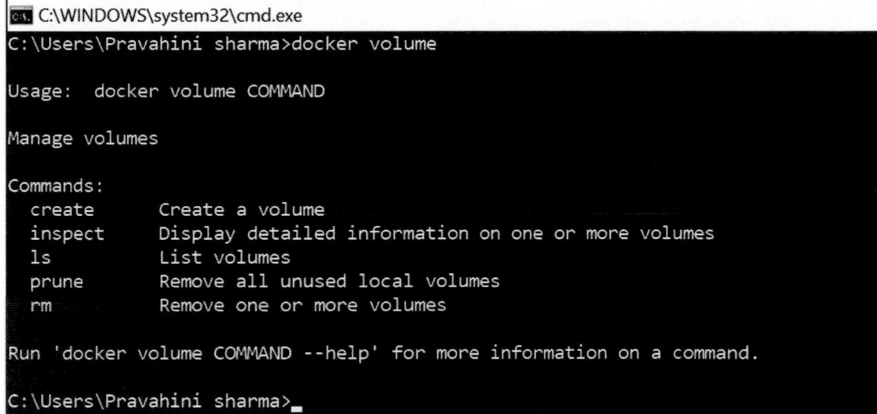

C:\WINDOWS\system32\cmd.exe
C:\Users\Pravahini sharma>docker volume
Usage: docker volume COMMAND
Manage volumes
Commands:
create Create a volume
inspect Display detailed information on one or more volumes
ls List volumes
prune Remove all unused local volumes
rm Remove one or more volumes
Run 'docker volume COMMAND --help' for more information on a command.
C:\Users\Pravahini sharma>_


**Figure 7.1** Docker volume command screenshot.

```
C:\WINDOWS\system32\cmd.exe

C:\Users\Pravahini sharma>docker volume create myvol1
myvol1

C:\Users\Pravahini sharma>
```

**Figure 7.2** Docker volume create command screenshot.

```
C:\Users\Pravahini sharma>docker volume ls
DRIVER    VOLUME NAME
local     2f0e053b141b456845dd82ed55460b76f85531565956511427ldd2fd059d10ec
local     4d8e1eb391e9a6506e8778fa03285850f2ca37b3ef49e6da65f33b5d0f819dfa
local     0324da2dbb7b32c57155aeb8350c705ba35d92b1b038fa4bff0d7a51bdd613ed
local     a8b6a201b6d17ddf8177e7c5751b2544c59d6a59d37fefa3e7338f65006fbc88
local     b7d3ad2fb0807dcde032a83006d53482bdcf9f670390f36c605a692019ff4305
local     b78cd43b776bc35a08e0b02625875256649f40cb88c84871d23f273954f5e0c1
local     c24c40b4f3cdafa3f4bd35668dd6c22511fc7d655a76f8c36d107bf1cb24de31
local     c956c060d8793646e730b10f5dfbc7a2371dbc2af70cd1c529ab9b5a36f70178
local     cb46c137ce30155bcc60cb3aa4d5e6f92b0ffee25f2647f654572ccd6d3d088c
local     d5b43952034220fdb7a4c7224e373ff256f802234abd4b31f84b6f2d7cc47c2f
local     e3cf1d156eb8a5e576e325b9586a3343c2d37ae5ce31dfd72db6c6281ef086f7
local     e69b59c3714b311f576192f6892b15fcd026f416fd26260fe40313013daddee7
local     f454f92132d76994aa2dfc84a4c7fcc0e815659b42d4ae486f202241b39f049d
local     myvol1

C:\Users\Pravahini sharma>
```

**Figure 7.3** Docker volume ls command screenshot.

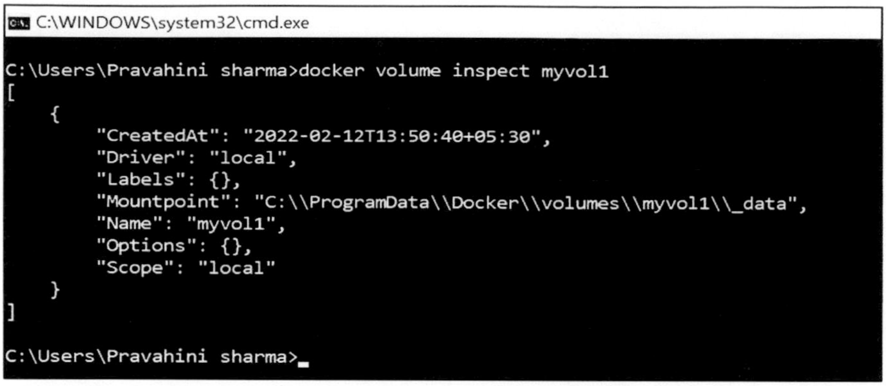

```
C:\WINDOWS\system32\cmd.exe

C:\Users\Pravahini sharma>docker volume inspect myvol1
[
    {
        "CreatedAt": "2022-02-12T13:50:40+05:30",
        "Driver": "local",
        "Labels": {},
        "Mountpoint": "C:\\ProgramData\\Docker\\volumes\\myvol1\\_data",
        "Name": "myvol1",
        "Options": {},
        "Scope": "local"
    }
]

C:\Users\Pravahini sharma>_
```

**Figure 7.4** Docker volume inspect command screenshot.

Note: here mountpoint means the volume is located at the given location and cannot be edited by the functions locally so the volume is secure.

- Docker volume rm <volume_name> : to remove volume.

### 7.5.4 Docker volume with Jenkins

Volumes are utilised to ensure that you do not lose your Jenkins information. On the off chance that you are utilising the - v banner on compartment creation (Docker holder run), go ahead and skirt this progression since Docker will consequently make the volume for you [9].

How it stores data using Jenkins:

- Creating a Jenkins container, we are going to use a named volume. Whenever we use named volume it is going to create volumes under /var/lib/docker/volumes/<volume_name>/_data
- This will get mapped in our Jenkins server where /var/Jenkins_home then we will configure our Jenkins server and create a job. Even though it gets deleted, our job-related information is stored over var/lib/docker/volumes/<volume_name>/_data
- Then we will create a new container if we attach this volume to a new container, we could able to see the content which we created in the previous Jenkins server.

#### 7.5.4.1 Create a Jenkins container

Command: docker run –name MyJenkins -v myvol1:/var/Jenkins_home -p 9090:8080 -p 60000:50000 jenkins/Jenkins (Figures 7.3–7.5).

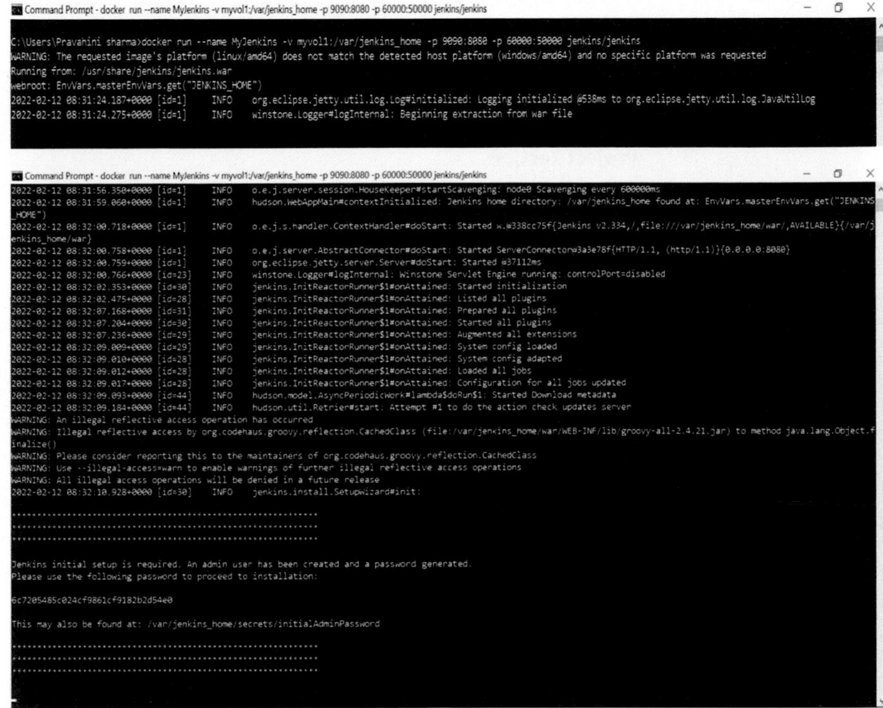


**Figure 7.5** Docker container for Jenkins.

## 7.5.4.2 Create a Jenkins test job on Jenkins console

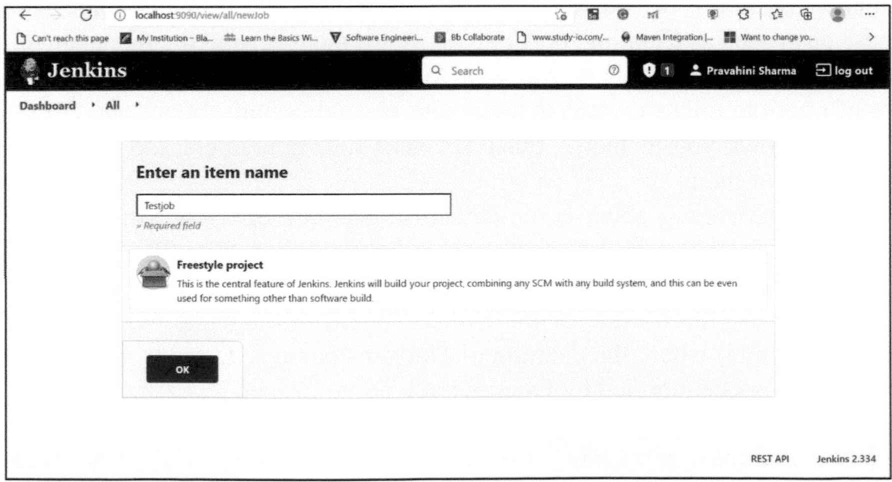


**Figure 7.6** Jenkins dashboard (create job window).

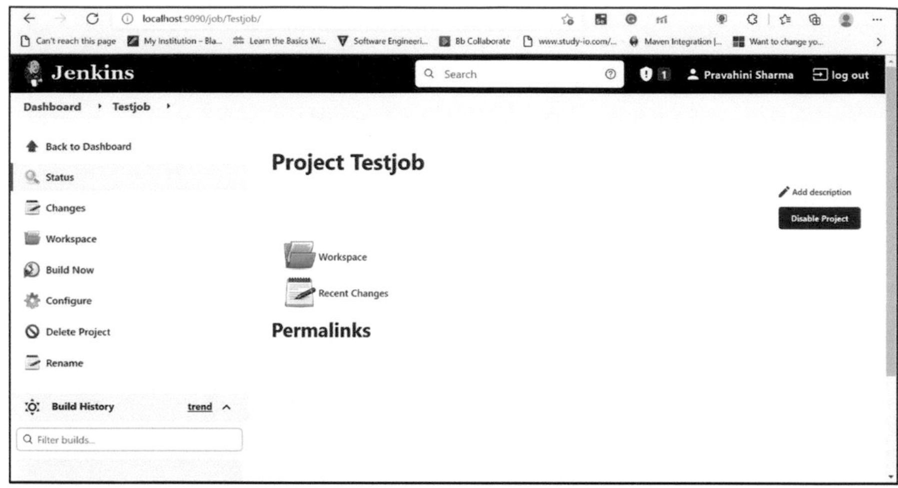


**Figure 7.7** Jenkins dashboard (job status window).

#### 7.5.4.3 Check for the job info on the container

Command: volume ls

docker inspect <volume_name> (Figures 7.6–7.8)

## 7.6 Docker Network

Docker is the PaaS model for creating and using containers on a tremendous level in many business companies today. At a big level, it is a mixture of Docker daemon processes and CLI. It solves common problems emerging these days such as Creating, port Publishing, removing, and the management of containers. It is the best ever tool for microservices, where you have a lot of multiple microservices that manage normal organisational operations; Docker allows you to merge those services into containers and simplifies packaging of them.

The network is about communication between different kinds of processes and Docker networking is not so different then this difference. The network in Docker is basically used to create the connections between Docker containers and the outside of the Docker world through the Main System (Host Machine) where the daemon of Docker operates. There is a vast variety of networks supported by Docker, each equal to specific case operations. We will be testing the network drivers that Docker often supports, as well as specific examples of coding. Docker networking completely differs from physical machines or VMs in some following ways.

```
C:\Users\Pravahini sharma>docker ps
CONTAINER ID   IMAGE     COMMAND   CREATED   STATUS    PORTS     NAMES

C:\Users\Pravahini sharma>docler ps -a
'docler' is not recognized as an internal or external command,
operable program or batch file.

C:\Users\Pravahini sharma>docker ps -a
CONTAINER ID   IMAGE             COMMAND                  CREATED          STATUS                             PORTS     NAMES
7348a8629275   jenkins/jenkins   "/sbin/tini -- /usr/…"   10 minutes ago   Exited (4294967295) 5 minutes ago            MyJenkins106
990bdd2cbb2c   jenkins/jenkins   "/sbin/tini -- /usr/…"   11 minutes ago   Created                                      MyJenkins107
6e3e51cd81a5   jenkins/jenkins   "/sbin/tini -- /usr/…"   11 minutes ago   Created                                      MyJenkins108
5e6b3ee95f31   jenkins/jenkins   "/sbin/tini -- /usr/…"   12 minutes ago   Created                                      MyJenkins109
24e9b56dea85   jenkins/jenkins   "/sbin/tini -- /usr/…"   22 minutes ago   Exited (4294967295) 5 minutes ago            MyJenkins
ea76d069f558   jenkins/jenkins   "/sbin/tini -- /usr/…"   24 minutes ago   Created                                      MyJenkins111
90e693740bf1   jenkins/jenkins   "/sbin/tini -- /usr/…"   26 minutes ago   Created                                      MyJenkins100
3d16b534ba64   jenkins/jenkins   "/sbin/tini -- /usr/…"   46 minutes ago   Exited (4294967295) 28 minutes ago           MyJenkins101
5ee2c362f33c   jenkins/jenkins   "/sbin/tini -- /usr/…"   46 hours ago     Created                                      MyJenkins12
fb252e9c37ce   jenkins/jenkins   "/sbin/tini -- /usr/…"   46 hours ago     Created                                      MyJenkins11
b6bc94bf4538   wordpress         "docker-entrypoint.s…"   47 hours ago     Exited (4294967295) 47 hours ago             upbeat_darwin
6fd46776469c   wordpress         "docker-entrypoint.s…"   2 days ago       Exited (4294967295) 46 hours ago             confident_chaplygin
fd78de5ccaf3   hello-world       "cmd /C 'type C:\\hel…"  2 days ago       Exited (0) 2 days ago                        sad_payne

C:\Users\Pravahini sharma>docker start 734
734

C:\Users\Pravahini sharma>docker ps
CONTAINER ID   IMAGE             COMMAND                  CREATED          STATUS         PORTS                                              NAMES
7348a8629275   jenkins/jenkins   "/sbin/tini -- /usr/…"   37 minutes ago   Up 2 minutes   0.0.0.0:9080->8080/tcp, 0.0.0.0:40000->50000/tcp   MyJenkins106

C:\Users\Pravahini sharma>_
```

```
C:\Users\Pravahini sharma>docker inspect 734
[
    {
        "Id": "7348a86292752e2b04ec63f0aad7d687ea36a21374f2173da630af3418f30ebf",
        "Created": "2022-02-12T08:43:09.4747767Z",
        "Path": "/sbin/tini",
        "Args": [
            "--",
            "/usr/local/bin/jenkins.sh"
        ],
        "State": {
            "Status": "running",
            "Running": true,
            "Paused": false,
            "Restarting": false,
            "OOMKilled": false,
            "Dead": false,
            "Pid": 306,
            "ExitCode": 0,
            "Error": "",
            "StartedAt": "2022-02-12T09:18:02.8250506Z",
            "FinishedAt": "2022-02-12T14:18:19.9572231+05:30"
        },
        "Image": "sha256:46c4fe2728d44987cfaa452f6ab412a4308a8e7fde54b04cf4b694f4324d98ad",
        "ResolvConfPath": "",
        "HostnamePath": "",
        "HostsPath": "",
        "LogPath": "C:\\ProgramData\\Docker\\containers\\7348a86292752e2b04ec63f0aad7d687ea36a21374f2173da630af3418f30ebf\\7348a86292752e2b04ec63f0aad7d687ea36a21374f2173da
630af3418f30ebf-json.log",
        "Name": "/MyJenkins106",
        "RestartCount": 0,
        "Driver": "lcow",
        "Platform": "linux",
        "MountLabel": "",
        "ProcessLabel": "",
        "AppArmorProfile": "",
        "ExecIDs": null,
        "HostConfig": {
            "Binds": [
                "myvol1:/var/jenkins_home"
            ],
            "ContainerIDFile": "",
```

**Figure 7.8** Docker container inspect command screenshot.

- Docker usually uses a bridge network, which is only available on Linux because it supports host networking. In this scope, virtual machines are a bit more flexible in some ways due to their great support with Host networking configuration and network address translation.
- Network isolation is achieved with the help of network namespace when using Docker containers but not the whole network stack.
- It is necessary for a host to support networking at a large scale so that thousands of processes (containers) can be created and run on a single Docker host system.

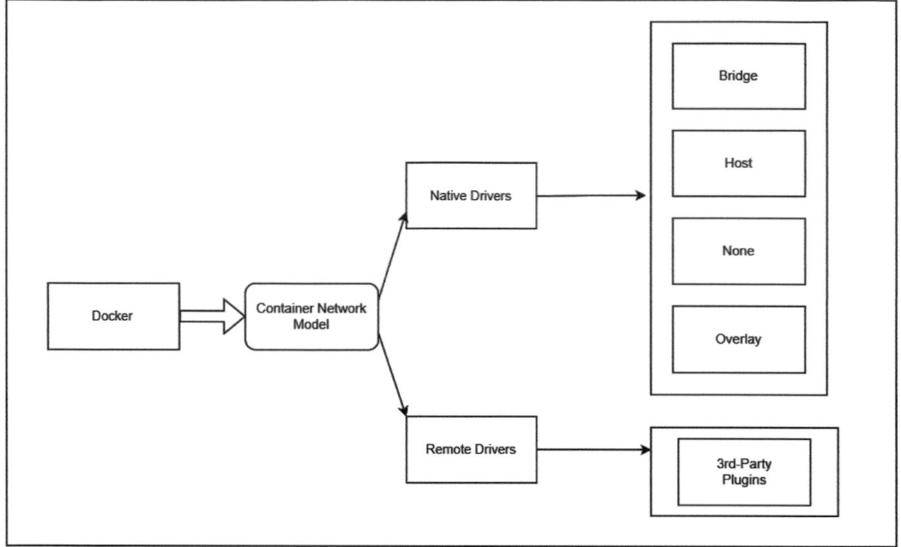


**Figure 7.9** Docker networks drivers.

### 7.6.1 Docker network drivers

Docker creates the default bridge connection to manage the connections between containers so that you do not need to waste time thinking about the connections and put your precious time into creating and using the containers. Though the default network works well in most cases, it is not the only way to create a network (Figure 7.9).

Creating the networks out of the box Docker provides three different ways to do so:

- Bridge
- Host
- None

Though all these three may not work with all operating conditions, we can also see user-defined networks such as the Macylan network and Overlay Network. Let us look into deep at each of these.

#### 7.6.1.1 Bridge driver

This network is created by default from Docker. When you run the Docker engine, all new containers that will be created will get connected automatically to the bridge network. You can use this network whenever you want

```
C:\Users\HP>docker network ls
NETWORK ID      NAME               DRIVER    SCOPE
989b4ea40916    Bantu              bridge    local
f8dacaafd82c    bridge             bridge    local
2ae2f8003d9f    dude               bridge    local
1cac19b4a585    host               host      local
859fe9c804ed    none               null      local
0360761aed17    practice_default   bridge    local

C:\Users\HP>
```

```
C:\Users\HP> docker run -dit --name busybox1 busybox /bin/sh
Unable to find image 'busybox:latest' locally
latest: Pulling from library/busybox
7e5209d2300f: Pull complete
Digest: sha256:34c3559bbdedefd67195e766e38cfbb0fcabff4241dbee3f390fd6e3310f5ebc
Status: Downloaded newer image for busybox:latest
235721d131fb4508d3905fbd04ec2f18549654678be8323addf1ad27aeec18f2

C:\Users\HP> docker run -dit --name busybox2 busybox /bin/sh
eb995cc0c16a5e4652d5541e5bf3d2bd4ca66f3cf1a149530ef67b0601cfb41a

C:\Users\HP>
```

**Figure 7.10** Docker network command output window.

the containers that you have created to work on their own to connect and communicate with the other containers. Since the containers work alone, the bridge network solves the problem of hole collision. Containers, which are connected to the same bridge network, can communicate with each other with the default bridge network. Only you need to specify the ports of the containers from which it has to be connected to the bridge network. For security and to prevent access from the outside of the bride network Docker uses iptables on the host machine (Figure 7.10):

1. To check available networks, we use *docker network ls*
2. Let us run two new containers from busybox named busybox 1 and busybox 2
3. To check whether the containers are fully up or not

   **Command:** *docker ps* (Figure 7.11)
4. Let us try to figure out whether the containers/container connected to the default bridge network or not (Figure 7.12)

   **Command:** *docker network inspect*

```
C:\Users\HP>docker ps
CONTAINER ID   IMAGE     COMMAND     CREATED              STATUS              PORTS     NAMES
eb995cc0c16a   busybox   "/bin/sh"   About a minute ago   Up About a minute             busybox2
235721d131fb   busybox   "/bin/sh"   About a minute ago   Up About a minute             busybox1

C:\Users\HP>_
```

**Figure 7.11** Docker running containers output window.

```
C:\Users\HP>docker network inspect bridge
[
    {
        "Name": "bridge",
        "Id": "f8dacaafd82c6eb8a391a7ae39522878ab819ed9152cfc07269254ad87b116b6",
        "Created": "2022-03-09T04:48:57.8652594Z",
        "Scope": "local",
        "Driver": "bridge",
        "EnableIPv6": false,
        "IPAM": {
            "Driver": "default",
            "Options": null,
            "Config": [
                {
                    "Subnet": "172.17.0.0/16",
                    "Gateway": "172.17.0.1"
                }
            ]
        },
        "Internal": false,
        "Attachable": false,
        "Ingress": false,
        "ConfigFrom": {
            "Network": ""
        },
        "ConfigOnly": false,
        "Containers": {
            "235721d131fb4508d3905fbd04ec2f18549654678be8323addf1ad27aeec18f2": {
                "Name": "busybox1",
                "EndpointID": "474ad28a43aabe7b7d9cf889cbb705c8b1ce0e43a204160499173ed9f9fa482d",
                "MacAddress": "02:42:ac:11:00:02",
                "IPv4Address": "172.17.0.2/16",
                "IPv6Address": ""
            },
            "eb995cc0c16a5e4652d5541e5bf3d2bd4ca66f3cf1a149530ef67b0601cfb41a": {
                "Name": "busybox2",
                "EndpointID": "907a929ca7c4374d4debbc0dc7f85d2dd996d299b4040f67adc0223b670c5f78",
                "MacAddress": "02:42:ac:11:00:03",
                "IPv4Address": "172.17.0.3/16",
                "IPv6Address": ""
            }
        },
        "Options": {
            "com.docker.network.bridge.default_bridge": "true",
            "com.docker.network.bridge.enable_icc": "true",
```

**Figure 7.12** Docker network inspect command output window.

5. Inside the network's inspect section you can find Container's section. There you can find out that there are two containers connected busybox 1 and busybox 2 with their Internet Protocol(ip) information. Let us try to ping busybox2 from busybox1 with ip address

```
C:\Users\HP>docker attach busybox1
/ # ping 172.12.0.3
PING 172.12.0.3 (172.12.0.3): 56 data bytes
^C
--- 172.12.0.3 ping statistics ---
55 packets transmitted, 0 packets received, 100% packet loss
/ # ping 172.17.0.3
PING 172.17.0.3 (172.17.0.3): 56 data bytes
64 bytes from 172.17.0.3: seq=0 ttl=64 time=0.123 ms
64 bytes from 172.17.0.3: seq=1 ttl=64 time=0.096 ms
64 bytes from 172.17.0.3: seq=2 ttl=64 time=0.096 ms
64 bytes from 172.17.0.3: seq=3 ttl=64 time=0.095 ms
64 bytes from 172.17.0.3: seq=4 ttl=64 time=0.096 ms
64 bytes from 172.17.0.3: seq=5 ttl=64 time=0.056 ms
64 bytes from 172.17.0.3: seq=6 ttl=64 time=0.096 ms
64 bytes from 172.17.0.3: seq=7 ttl=64 time=0.097 ms
64 bytes from 172.17.0.3: seq=8 ttl=64 time=0.102 ms
64 bytes from 172.17.0.3: seq=9 ttl=64 time=0.103 ms
^C
--- 172.17.0.3 ping statistics ---
10 packets transmitted, 10 packets received, 0% packet loss
round-trip min/avg/max = 0.056/0.096/0.123 ms
/ #
```

**Figure 7.13** Docker container attach command uutput window.

6. Remember that ping will only work when you pass the ip address of the other container not the name of the container (Figure 7.13).

The only drawback is that it is not beneficial for production because instead of the automatic service acquisition to resolve the Internet Protocol address in the name of the container, containers are linked to the IP address. A default bridge network is not a sustainable way to do it for applications which work in production because whenever you create or use a container a different IP address is assigned to that container which could be beneficial for locally driven development or for Continuous Integration and Continuous Delivery but certainly not for application to work in production. There is another strong reason why should we do not use the bridge network is that it also allows the containers to communicate with each other which has no relation among them which lead to a security vulnerability.

#### 7.6.1.2 Host driver

As you can guess through the name the host driver is the driver, which uses the host machine's network. With the host driver, there is no network partition between the host machine and the container where Docker operates. For example, suppose you are using a container with a port of 80 and using the host network for it, the application of that container will be available in port 80 to the host IP address.

```
C:\Users\HP>docker container run --publish 80:80 --name nginx_container nginx
/docker-entrypoint.sh: /docker-entrypoint.d/ is not empty, will attempt to perform configuration
/docker-entrypoint.sh: Looking for shell scripts in /docker-entrypoint.d/
/docker-entrypoint.sh: Launching /docker-entrypoint.d/10-listen-on-ipv6-by-default.sh
10-listen-on-ipv6-by-default.sh: info: Getting the checksum of /etc/nginx/conf.d/default.conf
10-listen-on-ipv6-by-default.sh: info: Enabled listen on IPv6 in /etc/nginx/conf.d/default.conf
/docker-entrypoint.sh: Launching /docker-entrypoint.d/20-envsubst-on-templates.sh
/docker-entrypoint.sh: Launching /docker-entrypoint.d/30-tune-worker-processes.sh
/docker-entrypoint.sh: Configuration complete; ready for start up
```

**Figure 7.14** Docker port mapping window.

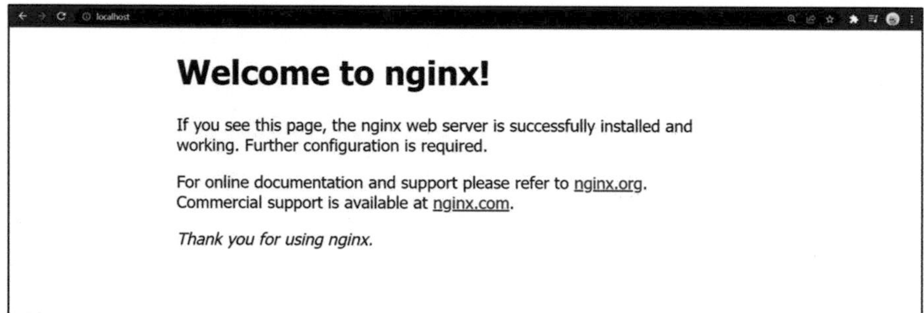

localhost
Welcome to nginx!
If you see this page, the nginx web server is successfully installed and working. Further configuration is required.
For online documentation and support please refer to nginx.org.
Commercial support is available at nginx.com.
Thank you for using nginx.


**Figure 7.15** Nginx container home page.

A host network is useful when you do not want to be dependent on the Docker network but want to rely on the host network. But here is also a drawback of the Host driver, it does not work with Docker Desktop (for Windows). For using the host network you need to use Docker in the Linux host machine. This chapter focuses on the Docker Desktop, but we will show you the instructions needed to work with a Linux host. The command below will create and start the container from the Nginx webserver image on port 80 available on the host machine (Figure 7.14).

**Command:** *Docker container run –publish 80:80 –name nginx_container nginx*

Accessing: localhost:80

The drawback of host networking is that you cannot use multiple with the same port in the same host system network (Figure 7.15).

#### 7.6.1.3 None driver

If you do not want to attach the container to any network so that container would not be able to access the external network as well as it would not be

```
C:\Users\HP>mkdir docker

C:\Users\HP>cd docker

C:\Users\HP\docker>docker swarm init
Swarm initialized: current node (jd3vwdu0227eaonl4d5bhcz3k) is now a manager.

To add a worker to this swarm, run the following command:

    docker swarm join --token SWMTKN-1-5zaz0aj4lw5myjv0707wdq13u660h3j3kh32tl5cwimqml2yty-8jya5yj9h2nmw9mga1fg1ix55 192.168.65.3:2377

To add a manager to this swarm, run 'docker swarm join-token manager' and follow the instructions.


C:\Users\HP\docker>docker network create -d overlay our-overlay-network
v7tn5w5e842ddu0n2wd72wndc

C:\Users\HP\docker>
```

**Figure 7.16** Overlay network command.

```
C:\Users\HP\docker>docker network create -d overlay --attachable mine-attachable-overlay
maort3h1ajv0yzt7998b79xeb

C:\Users\HP\docker>
```

**Figure 7.17** Overlay network command to connect.

able to communicate with other containers. None driver is useful if you do not want to connect the container to any network.

#### 7.6.1.4 Overlay driver

With overlay driver, containers can communicate with each other across the hosts for understanding the overlay driver. We can think overlay driver as a distributed network which goes across an existing computer network. The overlay driver is useful for multi-host networking like Kubernetes and Docker Swarm. Use the command below to create overlay network with Docker Swarm (Figure 7.16).

**Command**: *docker network create -d overlay our-overlay-network*
We use the command below for the creation of an overlay network with it standalone containers will be able to communicate with each other

**Command:**
*docker network create -d overlay –attachable mine-attachable-overlay* (Figure 7.17)

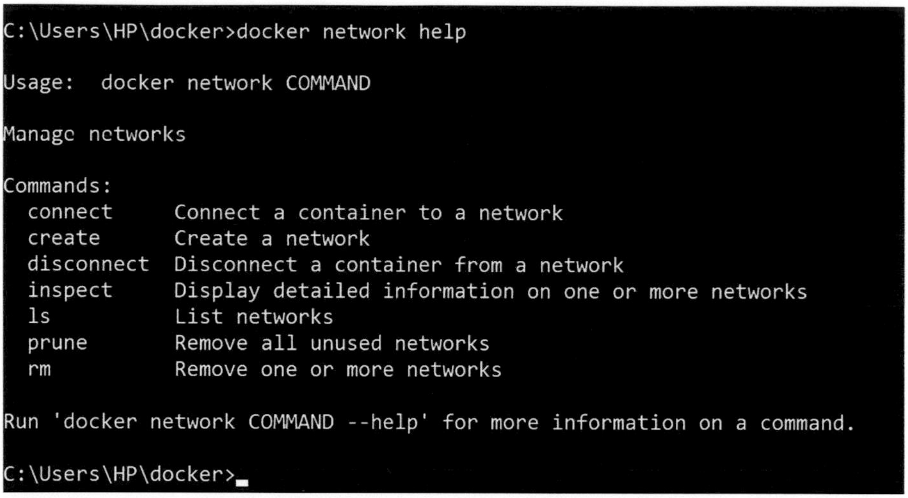

```
C:\Users\HP\docker>docker network help

Usage:  docker network COMMAND

Manage networks

Commands:
  connect     Connect a container to a network
  create      Create a network
  disconnect  Disconnect a container from a network
  inspect     Display detailed information on one or more networks
  ls          List networks
  prune       Remove all unused networks
  rm          Remove one or more networks

Run 'docker network COMMAND --help' for more information on a command.

C:\Users\HP\docker>_
```

**Figure 7.18** Network command output.

#### 7.6.1.5 Macvlan driver

According to Docker documents, Macvlan driver in Docker connects containers directly to the physical handling layer of the network. With a Macvlan driver, we assign a MAC address to the container, which makes it work like a portable device connected to your network. The containers directly interact with the network with their respective MAC addresses. It is a better choice when you have to work with legacy applications which are needed to be connected directly to the true network on their own. And it is a far better choice than delivering it through the Docker host network.

### 7.6.2 Basic Docker networking commands

To see the Docker network command list, use the *Docker network help* (Figure 7.18)

#### 7.6.2.1 Connecting a container to the network

Let us connect a container to network1, which we willl create (Figure 7.19).

Let us inspect the network.

#### 7.6.2.2 Disconnect a container from the network

**Command:** docker network disconnect <network_name> <container_id>

```
C:\Users\HP\docker>docker network inspect network1
[
    {
        "Name": "network1",
        "Id": "bd7bc057131a492ce2fadca6d1cced434ca5db0544a2ea411f348d8c14452592",
        "Created": "2022-03-09T05:47:37.462882Z",
        "Scope": "local",
        "Driver": "bridge",
        "EnableIPv6": false,
        "IPAM": {
            "Driver": "default",
            "Options": {},
            "Config": [
                {
                    "Subnet": "172.21.0.0/16",
                    "Gateway": "172.21.0.1"
                }
            ]
        },
        "Internal": false,
        "Attachable": false,
        "Ingress": false,
        "ConfigFrom": {
            "Network": ""
        },
```

**Figure 7.19** Network inspect command output.

*7.6.2.2.1 Removing a network*
**Command**: *docker network rm <network_name>*

*7.6.2.2.2 Removing all networks:*
**Command:** *docker network prune* (Figure 7.20)

### 7.6.2.3 Public networking

To make the containers IP and port address accessible to the outside Docker world, we need to publish it on a certain port for this we use -p or –publish and give the specific port.

**Command:**
*docker container run -d –publish 8080:80*
For the above command, we have mapped the container's TCP 80 port on 8080 on the Docker host.

### 7.6.2.4 Networking with Docker compose

It is a tool in Docker, which you would like for launching applications with multiple containers in Docker. In this tool, there is a docker-compose.yml file written in the YAML language. In this file, you can define the different kind of services which you want to start and their respective containers and their dependencies to start. If you do not mention then Docker-compose will connect all the containers which will start with a single network during the compilation (Figure 7.21).

```
C:\Users\HP\docker>docker network ls
NETWORK ID     NAME                       DRIVER    SCOPE
989b4ea40916   Bantu                      bridge    local
f8dacaafd82c   bridge                     bridge    local
a9392eff13a1   docker_gwbridge            bridge    local
2ae2f8003d9f   dude                       bridge    local
1cac19b4a585   host                       host      local
f2h90pxkimr5   ingress                    overlay   swarm
maort3h1ajv0   mine-attachable-overlay    overlay   swarm
859fe9c804ed   none                       null      local
v7tn5w5e842d   our-overlay-network        overlay   swarm
0360761aed17   practice_default           bridge    local

C:\Users\HP\docker>docker network prune
WARNING! This will remove all custom networks not used by at least one container.
Are you sure you want to continue? [y/N] y
Deleted Networks:
mine-attachable-overlay
our-overlay-network
practice_default
Bantu
dude
```

**Figure 7.20** Network prune command output.

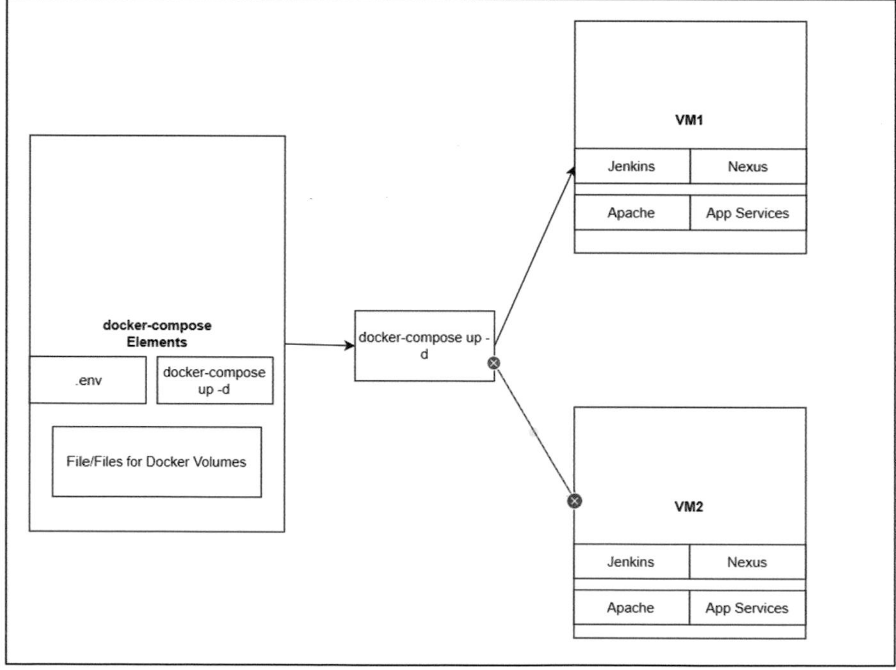


**Figure 7.21** Docker-compose flow.

```
push            Push service images
restart         Restart services
rm              Remove stopped containers
run             Run a one-off command
scale           Set number of containers for a service
start           Start services
stop            Stop services
top             Display the running processes
unpause         Unpause services
up              Create and start containers
version         Show version information and quit

[+] Running 0/1ker>docker compose -d
[+] Running 0/1
 - db Pulling                                                    8.7s

C:\Users\HP\docker>docker compose up -d
```

**Figure 7.22** Docker-compose up command output.

All the containers will connect through the default network. Let us peep in docker-compose.yaml file in this we have MySQL and WordPress image Docker-compose connects wordpress containers port-80 to the port-80 which is available in the host system and we have specified in the docker-compose.yml file. If we do not define any custom network Docker-compose will create one for you. Look at the image above the network called downloads_default is already created now.

To turn up the Docker-compose we use

**Command**: *docker-compose up -d*

The output shown above (Figure 7.22) displays the running output of multiple containers.

## 7.7 Conclusion

Docker volumes are a generally utilised and helpful device to guarantee information determination while chipping away at holders. Docker volumes document frameworks are introduced in Docker holders to store information created by the dynamic compartment. Volumes are the favoured instrument for continuing information produced by and utilised by Docker compartments. While tie mounts are reliant upon the catalog construction and OS of the host machine, volumes are totally overseen by Docker. Volumes enjoy a few upper hands over tie mounts. Likewise, volumes are frequently a preferred decision over persevering information in a compartment's writable layer. Because a volume does not expand the size of the holders utilising it, and the volume's substance exists outside the lifecycle of a given holder. On the off chance that your holder produces non-determined state information, consider utilising a tmpfs mount to try not to store the information anyplace forever, and to expand the compartment's presentation by trying not to compose into the holder's writable layer.

## References

[1] Ståhl, D. and Bosch, J. Modeling continuous integration practice differences in industry software development. Journal of Systems and Software, 87 (2014), 48–59.

[2] Hitesh Kumar Sharma; Anuj Kumar; Sangeeta Pant; Mangey Ram, "6 Application of Blockchain in Smart Healthcare," in Artificial Intelligence, Blockchain and IoT for Smart Healthcare , River Publishers, 2022, pp. 57–66.

[3] Hitesh Kumar Sharma; Anuj Kumar; Sangeeta Pant; Mangey Ram, "7 Security and Privacy challenge in Smart Healthcare and Telemedicine systems," in Artificial Intelligence, Blockchain and IoT for Smart Healthcare , River Publishers, 2022, pp. 67–76.

[4] Sharma, H. K., Khanchi, I., Agarwal, N., Seth, P., & Ahlawat, P. (2019). Real time activity logger: A user activity detection system. Int J Eng Adv Technol, 9(1), 1991–1994.

[5] Jabbari, R., bin Ali, N., Petersen, K. and Tanveer, B. What is DevOps?: A Systematic Mapping Study on Definitions and Practices. XP2016, ACM, 2016. [14] Walls, M. Building a DevOps Culture. O'Reily Medis, Inc., 2013.

[6] Sharma, H. K., Kumar, S., Dubey, S., & Gupta, P. (2015, March). Auto-selection and management of dynamic SGA parameters in RDBMS. In 2015 2nd International Conference on Computing for Sustainable Global Development (INDIACom) (pp. 1763–1768). IEEE.

[7] Sharma, H. K., Singh, S. K., & Ahlawat, P. (2014). Model-based testing: the new revolution in software testing. Database Syst J, 4(1), 26–31.

[8] Sharma, H. K., Jindal, M., Munjal, K., & Jain, A. (2017). An effective model of effort estimation for Cleanroom software development approach. ICRDSTHM-17) Kuala Lumpur, Malasyia.

[9] Kumar, A., Pant, S., Ram, M., & Yadav, O. (Eds.). (2022). Meta-heuristic Optimization Techniques: Applications in Engineering (Vol. 10). Walter de Gruyter GmbH & Co KG.

[10] Lwakatare, L. E., Kuvaja, P. and Oivo, M. Relationship of DevOps to Agile, Lean and Continuous Deployment: A Multivocal Literature Review Study. Springer, City, 2016.

# 8

# Container Orchestration: Managing Cluster of Containers

## Abstract

Handling multiple containers manually is a very difficult task. Creating and managing multiple containers required a well-managed platform which we called a container orchestration tool. Docker Swarm, Kubernetes, etc. are some important tools used for handling multiple containers together. Out of these tools, Kubernetes has a complete ecosystem for automatically managing the containers. In this chapter, we have explained container orchestration and the various platforms available for handling multiple containers.

## 8.1 Introduction

In real IT projects, a single container is not sufficient to fulfil the need of the business user. Multiple containers are required to run simultaneously to serve the service to business users. Container Orchestration is the process to monitor and control multiple containers together and provide a platform to communicate with each other. Today, Kubernetes and Docker Swarm are the most famous orchestration tool. Cloud suppliers including Amazon Web Services (AWS), Google Cloud Platform, IBM Cloud and Microsoft Azure offer oversaw Kubernetes administrations [1, 2]. A container is a bundling system that assists and allows running the microservice in an isolated manner.

In particular, a container incorporates all the executables, paired code, libraries, and arrangement records which are required to serve the dedicated service. As we have seen earlier, containers are more lightweight and proficient in comparison of VMs.

## 8.2 Container Orchestration

Whenever the number of containers increases significantly, container orchestration becomes an essential factor, particularly in the CI/CD pipeline [3]. Container Orchestration is an automated framework to monitor and control the overall processing of containers. It is remarkably difficult to oversee containers working without the contribution of container orchestration. Container Orchestration mostly focuses on the existing patterns of containers and their working elements. Container orchestration automates the arrangement, scaling and systems administration of containers. Container organization can be utilised in any environment where containers are used. It can assist you with conveying similar applications across various conditions without expecting to upgrade it. Furthermore, microservices in containers make it more straightforward to arrange administrations, including capacity, systems administration, and security. Containers give your microservice-based applications, an optimal container orchestration unit and independent execution climate [4].

Some major advantages of using Container Orchestration tools are given below:-

- **Wellbeing checks:** Container Orchestration tools are used to check the health of running containers in an automated manner. This toll regularly pings an active message to each container running in their environment and identify the activeness based upon the response received from the individual container.
- **Allocating resources:** Allocation of required resources for all containers, is also the main functionality of any Container Orchestration Tool.
- **Updates and re-configured:** Containers are redesign and update resources with zero downtime time. It is done in an automated manner by Orchestration Tool.
- **Discovering services**: This is the idea of how the microservices or applications find each other in the organisation. It assists the clients with diminishing the design exertion required in setting up the cycle. It is also a core task of an Orchestration tool.

## 8.3 Need for Container Orchestration

Assume four applications are running in a similar language, OS, and server. You are an administrator attempting to physically deploy, scale, and upgrade the security of the entire framework to ensure everything is running as per the required expectations. Scaling containers across the business is a challenging task without automated tools. Container Orchestration can manage these tasks very efficiently. The work is consequently performed without human intervention so that the scaling of the application is executed effectively.

Here are some additional advantages of using container orchestration:-

- **Rearrange and speedup activities:** Orchestration tools are helpful for rearranging and fast allocation of resources. These tools do these tasks in an automated manner, so compared to manual allocation it is faster.
- **Upgrades versatility:** These tools are also helpful for updating the requirements of the running containers in an automated manner.
- **Enhance security:** Container orchestration diminishes human mistakes and outside dangers.

Container orchestration is utilised to automate the following tasks:-

- Arranging and booking of containers.
- Provisioning and organisation of containers.
- Accessibility of containers.
- The setup of utilisations as far as the containers that they run in.
- Scaling of containers to similarly adjust application responsibilities across the foundation.
- Distribution of resources between containers.
- Load adjusting, traffic steering and administration disclosure of containers.
- Well-being checking of containers.
- Getting the collaborations between containers.

Scalability is the issue that containerisation settles while confronting functional difficulties in using containers. The issue starts when there are numerous containers and services to oversee all the while. Their association becomes convoluted and bulky. Containers orchestration tackles that issue by offering functional strategies for mechanising the administration, organisation, scaling, systems administration, and accessibility of containers.

Microservices use containerisation to provide more adaptable and agile applications [5, 6]. The Orchestration tool gives organisations complete admittance to a particular arrangement of resources, either in the physical or virtual working framework. It is the reason containerisation stages have become one of the most pursued platform for computerised change.

The amortisation of multiple containers includes:

- Container Provisioning
- Container Deployment
- Container overt repetitiveness and accessibility
- Eliminating or increasing containers to spread the heap equally across the host's framework
- Designating resources between containers
- Checking the wellbeing of containers and hosts
- Arranging an application according to explicit containers which are utilising them
- Adjusting administration revelation load between containers
- Aiding the development of containers starting with one host and then onto the next assuming assets are restricted or then again if a host terminates

To clarify how containerisation functions, we really want to check the organisation of microservices i.e. containerised application. Microservices utilise containerisation to convey single-work modules. They cooperate to create more versatile and coordinated applications. It saves time, assets, and considers adaptability the monolithic application cannot provide.

## 8.4 Working of Container Orchestration

Container orchestration conveys a few more advantages for handling multiple container. To capitalise on container orchestration, it is fundamental to completely comprehend the way it works.

Ordinarily, container orchestration tools require the application design in YAML or JSON [7, 8]. These records, explicitly, help orchestration tools to control multi-containerised application.

Kubernetes and Docker Swarm are the most famous tools for container orchestration. Configuration files are used by the container orchestration tools to organise among container. The orchestration tools additionally plan to send of containers into bunches and decide the best host for the container. After a host is chosen, the orchestration tools deal with the lifecycle of the container. The orchestration tools work in any climate that runs containers.

Orchestration tools are progressively well-known because of their flexibility. They can work in any climate, which upholds containers. In this way, they support both conventional on-premise servers and public cloud occasions, running on administrations like Microsoft Azure or Amazon Web Services.

## 8.5 Container Orchestration Tools

### 8.5.1 Kubernetes

Kubernetes is a well-known orchestration tool that utilise a DevOps approach and it also provides the functionality for cloud administrations including AWS, IBM, Microsoft, Intel, and Cisco.

#### 8.5.1.1 Benefits

Kubernetes is broadly valued for its motility. Jobs can be moved without rethinking the application or foundation. Kubernetes makes a theoretical equipment layer that permits DevOps groups to convey platform-as-a-service (PaaS), and makes it simpler to demand extra assets to scale an application without the requirement for more actual machines [9].

#### 8.5.1.2 Challenges

Kubernetes can be trying because of its boundlessness framework. Supplemental innovations and administrations are frequently important to convey a start-to-finish arrangement. Security is another test, particularly for huge ventures. Assuming a solitary Kubernetes bunch is undermined by a programmer, different groups might become helpless too [10].

### 8.5.2 Docker swarm

Docker Swarm is more clear and less popular than Kubernetes. But it is helpful for programming advancement groups. The completely coordinated Docker holder arrangement instrument is known as Docker Swarm and gives a less difficult way to container sending.

#### 8.5.2.1 Benefits

Assuming you are working on various cloud stages or then again if you are new to container organisation, Docker Swarm is an engaging arrangement stage because of convenience and a low expectation to absorb information. Docker Swarm is an optimal decision for more modest orchestrations. Docker is likewise notable for giving and keeping up with refreshed documentation, which is useful.

#### 8.5.2.2 Challenges

Probably the best drawback of Docker Swarm is the absence of a choice to associate containers to capacity. Docker Swam is less flexible in comparison to Kubernetes. One more deterrent for some is that Docker Swarm upholds Windows and Mac OS X, yet utilises virtual machines to run on non-Linux stages [7, 9]. Thus, assuming an application is intended for a Windows-based Docker container. It is not viable with Linux, dissimilar to Kubernetes administration which is not dependent on the working framework.

### 8.5.3 Apache Mesos

Apache Mesos was initially evolved at UC Berkeley. It was taken on for use by enormous undertakings including Uber, Yelp, AirBnb, Twitter, and Paypal. Mesos has a particular design and can deal with an expansive scope of responsibilities because of 'use mindful' planning.

#### 8.5.3.1 Benefits

Mesos enjoys many benefits, including its lightweight point of interaction and backing of various programming dialects. It additionally works on asset allotment by joining unique information assets into a solitary pool without influencing execution. The best advantage of Mesos is its innate adaptability and versatility. You can without much of a stretch, scale an application or framework to a huge number of nodes.

#### 8.5.3.2 Challenges

Mesos is not really a container orchestration tool, it essentially gives a bunch of the board. Compartment arrangement is one of the numerous jobs that can run on top of Mesos because of its Marathon system, which offers holder organisation as a component. Quite possibly the main hindrance to carrying out Mesos is its high expectation to learn and adapt. It is probably going to require specialisation and specialised skills. While it is a fitting decision for enormous-scope undertakings, it could be pointless excess for more modest associations with restricted tech assets [5, 9].

## 8.6 Docker Swarm Container Orchestration Versus Kubernetes Container Orchestration

Kubernetes and Docker are the two current market pioneers in building and overseeing containers. Docker, when originally opened, became inseparable from containerisation. A runtime climate makes and fabricates programming inside containers. As per Statista, more than half of IT pioneers detailed involving Docker container innovation in their organisations last year. Kubernetes is a container orchestrator. It perceives numerous container runtime conditions, like Docker.

The following are some Docker orchestration tools:

- **Docker machine** – Installs Docker Engine and sets up hosts.
- **Docker swarm** – Groups several Docker hosts into a single container. It is also compatible with any tool that uses a single Docker host.
- **Docker compose** – Creates the containers needed to deploy multi-container applications.

The following features are included in Kubernetes orchestration tools:

- Container deployment and replication are automated.
- Container clusters can be scaled in or out in real time.
- Load balancing container groupings.
- Failed containers are automatically rescheduled.
- Network ports are exposed to systems outside of the cluster in a controlled manner.

To comprehend the distinctions between Kubernetes and Docker Swarm, we ought to analyse them even more intently. Each has its own orchestrations of benefits and hindrances, which makes the assignment of picking between one of them, an extreme one. To be sure, both advances contrast in a few central ways, as proven below (Table 1).

## 8.7 Some Other Container Orchestration Tools

- Google Container Engine (GKE): Google Container Engine is based on Kubernetes and works with running and the executives of containers on the Google Cloud.
- Red Hat Advanced Cluster Management for Kubernetes: GA the executive orchestration made to oversee half-breed cloud-local applications running in containers' conditions. Gives perceivability, strategy administration and control for containerised conditions.

**Table 8.1** Comparison of Docker swarm and Kubernetes.

| Keys to differentiate | Kubernetes | Docker Swarm |
|---|---|---|
| Setting up the container: | Docker Compose or Docker CLI cannot characterise containers. Kubernetes rather utilises its own YAML, client definitions, and API. These contrast from standard Docker equivalents. | The Docker Swarm API offers a significant part of the similar usefulness of Dockers, although it does not perceive Docker's orders as a whole. |
| High availability: | Pods are disseminated among nodes, offering high accessibility as it endures the disappointment of an application. Load-adjusting administrations recognise undesirable units and annihilate them. | Docker Swarm additionally offers high accessibility as the administrations can recreate through swarm hubs. The whole bunch is overseen by Docker's Swarm administrator hubs, which additionally handle the assets of specialist hubs. |
| Balancing load: | In many cases, an entrance is important for load-adjusting purposes. | A DNS component inside Swarm hubs can circulate approaching solicitations to an assistance name. These administrations can run on ports characterised by the client, or be allocated naturally. |
| Scalability/versatility: | Since Kubernetes has a complete and complex structure, it will in general give solid certifications about a brought-together arrangement of APIs as well as the group state. This arrangement eases back downscaling and deployment. | Docker Swarm deploys compartments a lot quicker, permitting quicker response times for accomplishing versatility. |
| Definition of application: | Applications convey in Kubernetes through a blend of microservices, units, and deployments. | Applications send either as microservices or as series in a multitude group. Docker-make helps in introducing the application. |
| Networking: | Kubernetes has a level systems administration model. This orchestration permits all cases to collaborate with one another as indicated by network particulars. To do such, it carries out as an overlay. | As a hub joins a multitude group, an overlay organisation will create. This overlay network covers each host in the Docker Swarm, alongside a host-just Docker span organisation. |

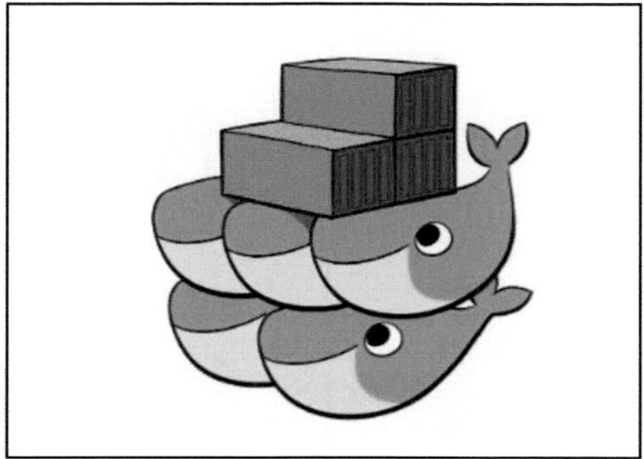

**Figure 8.1** Docker Swarm tool.

- Red Hat Quay: A container and application library giving secure stockpiling, conveyance, and arrangement of containers on any framework. Red Hat Quay.io is a facilitated adaptation of Red Hat Quay.
- CoreOS Fleet's Tectonic: This container is the executive's device that allows you to convey Docker compartments, and has in a bunch as well as appropriate administrations across a group and has been incorporated with Red Hat.
- Cloud Foundry's Bosh is a cloud-skeptic open-source instrument for discharge designing, arrangement, and lifecycle of the executives of intricate appropriated frameworks.
- Cloud Foundry's KubeCF: It is an application runtime for Kube.

## 8.8 Docker Swarm

Docker Swarm is a container management tool that runs only on Docker applications. It helps end-clients in making and conveying a cluster of Docker nodes (Figure 8.1).

Every node of a Docker Swarm is a Docker daemon, and all Docker daemons collaborate by utilising the Docker API. Every container within the Swarm can be deployed and accessed by nodes of a similar cluster (Figure 8.2).

The following are five basic components inside a specialist environment:

- Docker images
- Docker container

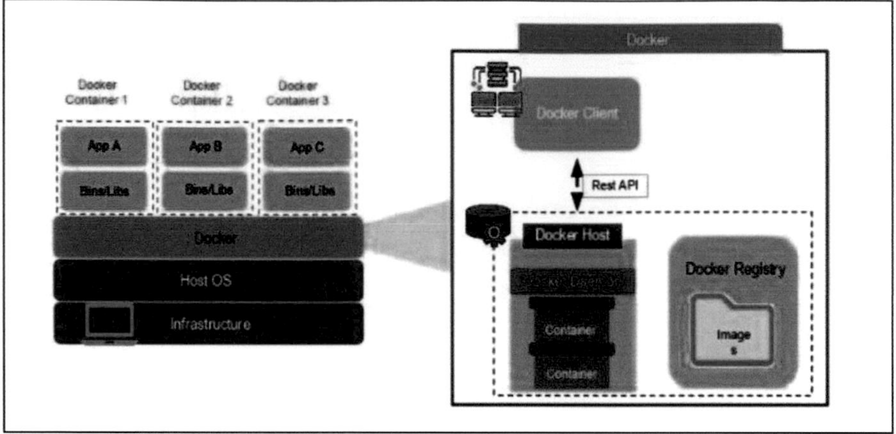


**Figure 8.2** Docker Swarm architecture.

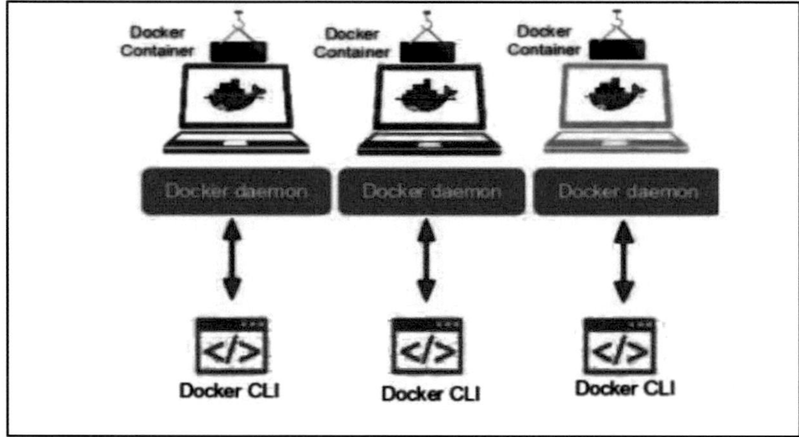


**Figure 8.3** Multi-container environment.

- Docker daemon
- Docker registry
- Docker client

Environment containing containers are shown below (Figure 8.3):

Docker Swarm can be considered for the use of making clusters and act as a scheduling tool offering many functionalities for the Docker.

Workload balancing is provided by the Docker Swarm which assigns the containers to the nodes and resources are being optimised by automatically scheduling on the most appropriate hosts. A swarm manager helps in the management and controls the swarm which is usually used in scheduling the container workloads. Docker Swarm images can be created for use as a service discovery token. Containers containing the Redis server on mostly all the swarm nodes. Contribution to the new stack computation that is placed on the assets of the virtualisation. It can be considered a daemon, which can keep on running on the non-terminating circle or loop and can act in charge of gathering and sending them to the API servers. The replication, administration account and endpoint controllers are the main key controllers. The proxy service of Kubernetes, which runs in every hand aids in the formation or generation of the administrations, which can be made accessible and can be given access to the outer host. With the help of the clusters of the container introduces the principles of security related to the cloud technology, which are availability, confidentiality and integrity. Docker is a platform as a service which generally involves the Amazon Web Services Elastic Beanstalk, OpenShift or Dooku. Because of the delayed services provided by the platform as a service we had to shift to the Docker containers from the virtual machines in many infrastructures as a service layer. The one having the webservers installed in their pcs and laptops, where the computing platforms or the virtual servers are completely isolated from the host. A container image which is known as a lightweight, stand-alone, executable package software piece including everything it needs such as code, runtime, system tools, system libraries and settings. Multiple storage services are used for both replications of the data and for stripping of the data. Docker Swarm Manager is used for sending the plain text which runs the Docker cryptography container.

Transfer of data takes place from the gateway manager to another storage containing the new node along with the multiple containers of Docker, which forms a storage cluster. Then the distribution of the encrypted data takes place. Multiple Docker containers would be storing the encrypted files. The following diagram shows the exact working model using Dockers for the security of the data it involves in Kubernetes. Kubernetes is a very proficient and efficient tool rather than the Docker Swarm. A Docker Swarm is for choosing those machines that will be executing a container. For satisfying the goal Docker Swarm principle is described in two phases. The first one is that with the help of the filter methods we are performing machine filtering.

There are in total 6 filters. They are as follows:

- Three node filters (constraint, health and container slots).
- Three configuration filters (affinity, dependency and port).

On starting the Docker Swarm Manager, it starts all the filters available and accessible and specifies filter subsets with the options – filter flag. Unhealthy nodes have been ignored for not running the containers.

Three types of container filters that can be used are as follows:

**Affinity filter:** Following affinities are being used as follows container ID/ name, host image and the custom label given to the container.

**Dependency filter:** It is generally used for co-scheduling the dependent containers on the same host.

**Port filter:** If the container does not occupy any other port, then that port gets selected by the swarm which is enabled.

Dependency filter step helps Port filter step to determine the strategy for efficient running of a container on docker swarm. The three strategies that swarm contains are **Spread, Bipack** and **Random**. Swarm manager uses the tag option strategy for scheduling the clusters in the clusters. Swarm uses the spread by default if none of the others is being specified. Instead of having so much of advantages of the strategies used by Docker Swarm some constraints are still there such as all the users are having the same priority which are having no differences between users. For the creation of several containers, it does not manage several requests. The CPU number which must include this we are making is set by the user itself. In the Docker Swarm cluster, we create a monitor. Docker Swarm cannot accept multiple requests for creating containers at the same time.

### 8.8.1 Features of Docker swarm

**Decentralised access:** Swarm makes it extremely simple for teams to access and manage the environment.

**High security:** Any communication between the manager and client nodes within the Swarm is profoundly secure.

**Autoload balancing:** There is autoload balancing within the environment and you can script that into how you work out and structure the Swarm environment.

### 8.8.2 Working with Docker swarm

- Initialise Swarm Mode using **Docker Swarm init** command (Figure 8.4).

```
Terminal Host 1  +

$ docker swarm --help

Usage:  docker swarm COMMAND

Manage Swarm

Commands:
  ca          Display and rotate the root CA
  init        Initialize a swarm
  join        Join a swarm as a node and/or manager
  join-token  Manage join tokens
  leave       Leave the swarm
  unlock      Unlock swarm
  unlock-key  Manage the unlock key
  update      Update the swarm

Run 'docker swarm COMMAND --help' for more information on a command.
$
```

```
Terminal Host 1  +
$ docker swarm init
Swarm initialized: current node (m7zqm4rhkssjgy4zix4lu9hsx) is now a manager.

To add a worker to this swarm, run the following command:

    docker swarm join --token SWMTKN-1-01wx7z5ai641k4byzwyro5j12gv4f6ue8fofkydea
zedd1xmr3-2nh55mrta88fou4vh3zkt0klp 172.17.0.53:2377

To add a manager to this swarm, run 'docker swarm join-token manager' and follow
 the instructions.

$ 
```

**Figure 8.4** Docker Swarm connectivity commands.

- Join Cluster using the following command. **Docker Swarm join --token SWMTKN-12j2wv9h4lf43rn90vr7xotbmjknlw35t6xia1ze5ehefvk8 3wlc10hxx4whp75nauydcbssurdy 172.17.0.39:2377 (Figure 8.5)**
- Create Overlay Network using the **Docker network** command.
- Deploy Service using the **Docker service** command.
- Inspect the State using the commands given below.
- For Final Scale Service use the Docker service scale command.

## 8.9 Conclusion

Container orchestration automates monitoring, controlling and systems administration of containers. Container organisation can be utilised in any environment where you use containers. It can assist you with conveying similar applications across various conditions without expecting to upgrade it.

```
Terminal Host 2

$ token=$(ssh -o StrictHostKeyChecking=no 172.17.0.53 "docker swarm join-token -q worker") && echo $token
Warning: Permanently added '172.17.0.53' (ECDSA) to the list of known hosts.
SWMTKN-1-01wx7z5ai641k4byzwyro5j12gv4f6ue8fofkydeazeddlxmr3-2nh55mrta88fou4vh3zkt0klp
$ docker swarm join 172.17.0.53:2377 --token $token
This node joined a swarm as a worker.
$
```

```
Terminal Host 1 +
$ docker node ls
ID                                  HOSTNAME          STATUS          AVAILABILI
TY          MANAGER STATUS          ENGINE VERSION
m7zqm4rhkssjgy4zix4lu9hsx *         host01            Ready           Active
            Leader                  19.03.13
55hd0z664q455cx7nmi3hbk60           host02            Ready           Active
                                    19.03.13
$
```

**Figure 8.5** Docker Swarm join manager command.

Furthermore, microservices in containers make it more straightforward to arrange administrations, including capacity, systems administration, and security. Containers give your microservice-based applications an optimal container orchestration unit and independent execution climate. They make it conceivable to run numerous pieces of an application autonomously in microservices, on similar equipment, with a lot more noteworthy command over individual pieces and life cycles.

## References


[1] Runeson, P. and Höst, M. Guidelines for conducting and reporting case study research in software engineering. Empirical software engineering, 14, 2 (2009), 131. Pant, S., Kumar, A., Ram, M., Klochkov, Y., & Sharma, H. K. (2022). Consistency Indices in Analytic Hierarchy Process: A Review. Mathematics, 10(8), 1206.

[2] Claps, G. G., Svensson, R. B. and Aurum, A. On the journey to continuous deployment: Technical and social challenges along the way. Information and Software technology, 57 (2015), 21–31.

[3] Hitesh Kumar Sharma; Anuj Kumar; Sangeeta Pant; Mangey Ram, "9 Methodologies for Improving the Quality of Service and Safety of Smart Healthcare," in Artificial Intelligence, Blockchain and IoT for Smart Healthcare , River Publishers, 2022, pp. 85–94.

[4] Hitesh Kumar Sharma; Anuj Kumar; Sangeeta Pant; Mangey Ram, "10 Cloud Commuting Platform for Smart Healthcare and Telemedicine," in

Artificial Intelligence, Blockchain and IoT for Smart Healthcare , River Publishers, 2022, pp. 95–104.

[5] Hitesh Kumar Sharma; Anuj Kumar; Sangeeta Pant; Mangey Ram, "11 Smart Healthcare and Telemedicine Systems: Present and Future Applications," in Artificial Intelligence, Blockchain and IoT for Smart Healthcare , River Publishers, 2022, pp. 105–116.

[6] Sharma, H. K., Kumar, S., Dubey, S., & Gupta, P. (2015, March). Auto-selection and management of dynamic SGA parameters in RDBMS. In *2015 2nd International Conference on Computing for Sustainable Global Development (INDIACom)* (pp. 1763–1768). IEEE.

[7] Sharma, H. K., Singh, S. K., & Ahlawat, P. (2014). Model-based testing: the new revolution in software testing. *Database Syst J*, *4*(1), 26–31.

[8] Sharma, H. K., Shastri, A., Biswas, R., & Singh, S. K. (2014). SGA Dynamic Parameters: The Core Components of Automated Database Tuning. *Database Systems Journal*, *5*(2), 13–21.

[9] Sharma, H. K., Jindal, M., Munjal, K., & Jain, A. (2017). An effective model of effort estimation for Cleanroom software development approach. *ICRDSTHM-17) Kuala Lumpur, Malasyia.*

[10] Kumar, A., Pant, S., Ram, M., & Yadav, O. (Eds.). (2022). Meta-heuristic Optimization Techniques: Applications in Engineering (Vol. 10). Walter de Gruyter GmbH & Co KG.

[11] PuppetLabs and DORA 2017 State of DevOps Report. City, 2017. [6] Roche, J. Adopting DevOps practices in quality assurance. Communications of the ACM, 56, 11 (2013), 38–43.

# 9

# Kubernetes: An Advanced Orchestration Platform


## Abstract

Container Orchestration is needed for the management of multiple containers in an automated manner. In a real-time production environment, we have to start multiple containers for multiple microservices. Manual checking of the health of these containers is not possible. Start/Stop/Suspend/Resume all these states could not be checked manually at run time for such a large number of containers. Kubernetes is one of the most useful tools donated by Google for container orchestration. In this chapter, we have explained the architecture of Kubernetes and the components in the Kubernetes ecosystem.


## 9.1 Introduction

To understand the need for a tool such as Kubernetes, we should understand how the deployment of applications took place. We have two options while deploying our application. One of them is the traditional method wherein various applications are deployed on the same physical server in a data centre. This requires a lot of maintenance such as that for the operating system and code. The second option is through deploying the code on virtual machines. According to the first scenario, when there is an application running on multiple machines, there might arise a scenario that the configuration of all the machines might not be consistent. Due to this reason when we deploy the code, it might not work very efficiently. This will result in errors within the infrastructure of all the environments and other problems with the uptime as well. The resource allocation to all the applications might not be done very efficiently. Thus, our application might not have proper support for load balancing across all the environments. Now if only one piece of software is stored on one piece of hardware, many resources of the server machine will not be utilised. Talking about the second scenario of using virtual machines, they provide us with better resource utilisation, scalability and also less cost because, through this architecture, we can also run various virtual machines on a single piece of hardware. However, this approach comes with its own disadvantages in that there may be potential security risks such as data breaches, and non-availability of resources as they may be used by some other application at that instance of time. It may also become very time-consuming. This will not only lead to the underconsumption of resources but also result in high costs as well. It is also important that we understand the difference between the two types of architectures, that is, monolithic architecture and microservices architecture that can be used for deploying applications. Monolithic applications are those types of applications wherein there is only one single codebase that has all the functionalities of the project inside it. The application is then deployed as a single jar or war file as per the use case. Even though this is an approach that is easy to follow, and deploy. However, it has various disadvantages. The size of the applications keeps on growing with time along with the coupling. It becomes difficult to understand and modify a particular functionality without affecting other parts of the code [1, 2].

Microservices architecture, on the other hand, focuses on an approach wherein the application is made up of smaller services that interact with each other using the http protocol. Each of the individual services has its own database, which proves to be highly beneficial because a database can be used that best fits the needs of that particular service. Through this approach, the applications become loosely coupled because of which changing any part of the application or functionality at a later point in time becomes a much simpler task. Through this, even if one part of the functionality stops working, the rest of them still continue to work as per requirement.

## 9.2 Kubernetes

It is an open-source platform that helps us to manage and deploy the containerised version of applications or a group of containers. Going back to the history of Kubernetes, it was introduced at Google as a project, which was reintroduced in 2014 as an open-source project so that everyone can benefit from it. Currently, the Cloud-Native computing foundation maintains Kubernetes [3].

### 9.2.1 Virtual machines versus Kubernetes

Kubernetes is a more secure platform than virtual machines when it comes to security. When it comes to portability, virtual machines also provide this functionality, however, Kubernetes provide much easier portability as they can work on any platform or environment. The overall time required for performing operations is much less in Kubernetes when compared to virtual machines as Kubernetes allows automatic allocation of resources to nodes as per requirement. The level of isolation is less in virtual machines when compared to Kubernetes because every virtual machine installed over the hypervisor has its own operating system. This also allows Kubernetes to run various containers on a single machine/ single piece of hardware [4].

### 9.2.2 Advantages

- It is a 100% open-source application, which is compatible across various platforms and provides a high level of flexibility. Being an open source, anyone can contribute to it through a version control system such as GitHub [5, 6].
- Workload scalability is a benefit of Kubernetes as various new servers can be added or removed as per requirement almost instantly through an automatic process. Scaling and changing the number of running containers can be done very efficiently.
- Kubernetes is said to have high availability because it is highly reliable and can be made available in any physical environment.
- It is designed for deployment as we can script out the environment and make it a part of our DevOps model so that the demands of customers can be met. We can speed up the process of various phases, which are a part of the deployment pipeline, such as testing, managing and deploying.
- Load balancing and service discovery become a relatively easier task as an approach of distributing the network will be followed whenever the traffic load is high, so that the deployment can be stable.

## 9.3 Installation of Kubernetes

### 9.3.1 Update the repositories

- Sudo su
- Apt-get update

### 9.3.2 Turn off swap space

- Swapoff -a
- vi /etc/fstab

### 9.3.3 Update the hostname

- vi /etc/hostname

### 9.3.4 Note the IP address

- Ifconfig

### 9.3.5 Update the hosts file

- Vi /etc/hosts

### 9.3.6 Set a static IP address

- Vi /etc/network/interfaces

### 9.3.7 Install OpenSSH server (Figure 9.1)

```
tanishka@kmaster:~$ sudo apt-get install openssh-server
Reading package lists... Done
Building dependency tree... Done
Reading state information... Done
The following additional packages will be installed:
  ncurses-term openssh-client openssh-sftp-server ssh-import-id
Suggested packages:
  keychain libpam-ssh monkeysphere ssh-askpass molly-guard
The following NEW packages will be installed:
  ncurses-term openssh-server openssh-sftp-server ssh-import-id
The following packages will be upgraded:
  openssh-client
1 upgraded, 4 newly installed, 0 to remove and 239 not upgraded.
Need to get 1,346 kB of archives.
After this operation, 5,926 kB of additional disk space will be used.
Do you want to continue? [Y/n] y
```

**Figure 9.1** OpenSSH-server installation command.

### 9.3.8 Install curl (Figure 9.2)

```
root@kmaster:/home/tanishka# apt-get update && apt-get install -y apt-transport-https curl
Hit:1 https://download.docker.com/linux/ubuntu hirsute InRelease
Hit:2 http://dl.google.com/linux/chrome/deb stable InRelease
Hit:3 http://packages.microsoft.com/repos/code stable InRelease
Hit:4 http://apt.pop-os.org/proprietary hirsute InRelease
Hit:5 http://us.archive.ubuntu.com/ubuntu hirsute InRelease
Hit:6 http://us.archive.ubuntu.com/ubuntu hirsute-security InRelease
Hit:7 http://ppa.launchpad.net/system76/pop/ubuntu hirsute InRelease
Hit:8 http://us.archive.ubuntu.com/ubuntu hirsute-updates InRelease
Hit:9 http://us.archive.ubuntu.com/ubuntu hirsute-backports InRelease
Reading package lists... Done
Reading package lists... Done
Building dependency tree... Done
Reading state information... Done
curl is already the newest version (7.74.0-1ubuntu2.3).
The following NEW packages will be installed:
  apt-transport-https
0 upgraded, 1 newly installed, 0 to remove and 239 not upgraded.
```

**Figure 9.2** Curl installation command.

### 9.3.9 Install the required dependencies and packages (Figure 9.3)

```
root@kmaster:/home/tanishka# curl -s https://packages.cloud.google.com/apt/doc
/apt-key.gpg | apt-key add -
Warning: apt-key is deprecated. Manage keyring files in trusted.gpg.d instead
(see apt-key(8)).
OK
root@kmaster:/home/tanishka# cat <<EOF >/etc/apt/sources.list.d/kubernetes.list

deb https://apt.kubernetes.io/ kubernetes-xenial main

EOF
root@kmaster:/home/tanishka#
```

**Figure 9.3** Dependencies and package installation command.

### 9.3.10 Update the Kubernetes configuration (Figure 9.4)

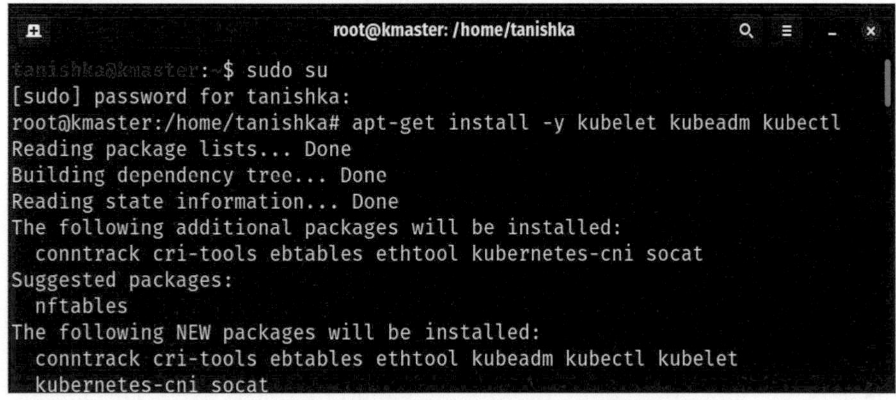

root@kmaster: /home/tanishka
:~$ sudo su
[sudo] password for tanishka:
root@kmaster:/home/tanishka# apt-get install -y kubelet kubeadm kubectl
Reading package lists... Done
Building dependency tree... Done
Reading state information... Done
The following additional packages will be installed:
conntrack cri-tools ebtables ethtool kubernetes-cni socat
Suggested packages:
nftables
The following NEW packages will be installed:
conntrack cri-tools ebtables ethtool kubeadm kubectl kubelet
kubernetes-cni socat


**Figure 9.4** Kubernetes configuration update command.

Figures 9.2–9.4 show the installation of some pre-requisite for Kubernetes.

After this step, add the following line to

/etc/systemd/system/kubelet.service.d/10-kubeadm.conf

→ Environment = "cgroup-driver=systemd/cgroup-driver=cgroupfs"

Thus, the installation is finally complete!

## 9.4 Companies using Kubernetes

When we talk about the applications of Kubernetes in the industry, various tech giants such as Google, Spotify, Pinterest, Tinder, etc. have started to incorporate Kubernetes into the architecture since 2015 *i.e* when Kubernetes was introduced as an open-source tool. It is no surprise that the organisation that created Kubernetes has been using it since it was launched. One significant point is that Google has made more than nine lakh contributions to the open-source Kubernetes project, which is more than any of the companies to date. Google has also introduced GKE (Google container engine) [7] through which we can deploy the Kubernetes application to the Google cloud, which will be discussed at greater length in the upcoming sections. Coming to the largest audio streaming platform with millions of subscribers, Spotify has shifted from its in-house orchestration system to Kubernetes since 2018. The company has experienced various benefits since then such as the scaling and orchestration of services have been done very efficiently to incorporate about 10 million requests per second. In addition, adding a new service to the production environment has been eased to a great extent. Similarly, sharing of millions of pictures takes place on the website and mobile application, which is developed by Pinterest. Thus, scaling and security of the containers that they are working on are necessary. Thus, adopting Kubernetes has proved to be highly beneficial for them, as according to reports and statistics about eighty percent of the resources are saved during non-peak hours.

### 9.4.1 Kubernetes on google cloud

GCP or the google cloud platform can be used for using the Kubernetes services at ease so that provisioning and maintenance can be done. However, for this to be possible, we require the Google Cloud Engine (GKE). This engine is particularly used because it offers various benefits such as repairing microservices after performing certain automatic health checks, logging essential data such as errors and other outputs and monitoring all the containers. Apart from the listed benefits, we can create clusters just by the click of a button. We can utilise the features of auto-repairing as well as auto-upgrading. It ensures that security does not take a backseat and offers to scan any potential vulnerabilities in the containers and offers encryption of data as well. One important point is that the underlying infrastructure of the cluster such as node pools, nodes, etc., can be automatically managed or managed by users as per their requirements. Thus, also this is a flexible feature which is provided by the GKE. The two modes can be particularly classified as Autopilot mode and Standard mode [8].

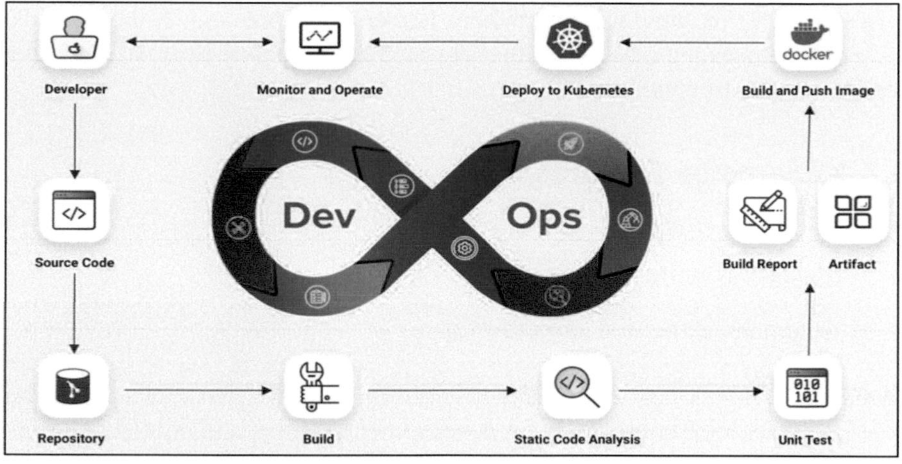


**Figure 9.5** DevOps various environment flowchart.

### 9.4.2 Kubernetes in DevOps pipeline

There are four stages in DevOps:

- Version Control: Source Code Management
- Continuous Integration: Continuous Builds
- Continuous Delivery: Continuous Testing
- Continuous Deployment: Configuration Management and containerisation

When a group of developers starts working on an application, the first problem they face is managing their source code, which is why we use GitHub as a source code management tool. Following that, a build is produced so that we may use tools like maven and Jenkins, which is a continuous integration tool. Jenkins is a Java-based open-source tool for automating software development and testing. Static code analysis and Junit testing are performed when the build is completed. After Junit is finished, a build report is generated (Artifact). These are part of the Build management and Continuous Integration categories (Figure 9.5).

In terms of continuous delivery and deployment, Docker is then used to containerise the build. Images may be easily shared and containerised. Each container is segregated from the others. Then, for container management, we will need a technology, which is where Kubernetes comes in. Kubernetes is a container management system that automates the deployment, scaling and load balancing of containers [9].

## 9.5 Kubernetes Features

- Automatic editing
- Livelihood skills
- Automatic extraction and retrieval
- Horizontal measurement and load balancing
- Provides local consistency for development, testing, and implementation
- Frequently integrated infrastructure in each component can serve as a separate unit
- Provides high density of resource utilisation
- Provides business-friendly features
- Central application request
- Automatic measurement infrastructure

Let us discuss some useful features of Kubernetes in detail:

- **Automatic bin packing:** When we deploy an application, we deploy it in a container. If we want that, a container automatically sees its resources and allocates the needed ones which can be done with the help of Kubernetes. Kubernetes automatically allocate all the required resources to the containers and uniformly distribute them across the cluster.
- **Load balancing:** Kubernetes can help containers in balancing the load or when one node of the cluster is down so to manage the cluster and its load helps.
- **Storage orchestration:** Kubernetes provides a platform or framework from where we can use storage solutions. Kubernetes mounts and adds a storage system of your choice to run apps
- **Self-healing:** If a node is down or a container is attempting to repair it, Kubernetes steps in to assist in the healing process.
- **Self-monitoring:** Kubernetes monitors the health of nodes and containers in real time.

- **Horizontal scaling:** Kubernetes allows you to easily and quickly measure resources not only directly but also horizontally.
- **Run anywhere:** Kubernetes is an open-source solution that allows you to run workloads on-premises, in a hybrid cloud, or in the cloud, allowing you to shift workloads wherever you wish.
- **Automatic rollouts:** If something goes wrong after you make a change to your app, Kubernetes will fix it for you.

## 9.6 Docker and Kubernetes

Docker is a container solution whereas Kubernetes is a container orchestration solution. Using Docker, we create the images. Containers are running instances of Docker images, but with the help of Kubernetes, we cannot create the containers. This is the big difference between them. Kubernetes is used to containerise the images but Docker is used to creating the images. Kubernetes is used to scale the containers; it is very robust and reliable. It has a huge community. Docker is used for automated building and deploying applications (CI) whereas Kubernetes is used for automated scheduling and management of application containers. Kubernetes provides an ecosystem for managing the Docker cluster [10].

They both are container orchestration solutions. Both are container orchestration tools, which automate deployment, load balancing and scaling of containers. Docker's native orchestration platform is called simply swarm. Since it is Docker's own orchestration platform, it came with lots of pros. One of the differences between Docker swarm and Kubernetes is if a container is made using Docker then only Docker swarm will work but Docker is not only an image builder tool, a container can be created by using any other tool so here Kubernetes works. So in simple words, we can say that Kubernetes works on all containers and Docker swarm works only for the container which is created using Docker.

- Learning Kubernetes is quite not easy, its installation and learning are complicated, whereas Docker swarm is easy to learn and fast to install. Kubernetes installation is complex while Docker swarm is easier.
- There is no graphical user interface (GUI) in Docker swarm but in Kubernetes, GUI is available [11].
- Let us talk about the scalability of Docker swarm vs Kubernetes. Scaling is faster in Docker swarm but cluster strength is not as robust. Whereas

scaling up is slow compared to swarm in Kubernetes but it guarantees a strong cluster state.

- Load balancing is a challenge maximum containers face. Load balancing requires manual service configuration in K8S whereas Docker swarm provides a built-in load-balancing technique.
- K8S has inbuilt logging & monitoring tools whereas only third-party logging and monitoring tools are used in Docker swarm.
- Kubernetes needs a separate CLI tool whereas Docker Swarm integrates Docker CLI.
- In Docker, swarm scaling is done manually whereas in Kubernetes auto-scaling is done. Whenever there is high traffic Kubernetes will auto-scale the containers.
- Kubernetes is more powerful than Docker swarm; also it has more community online.

Kubernetes is by default industry leader, there are many advantages to Kubernetes. It is very robust, very scalable, and very reliable. In Spite of that, Docker swarm is easy to learn, and install.

## 9.7 Kubernetes Play Pokemon Go: A Case Study of Pokemon Go

Pokemon Go is a game played by millions of users. It is an augmented reality game developed by Niantic for Android & iOS devices. Pokemon Go has 500+ million downloads, and 20+ million daily active users. Inspired users to walk over 5.4 billion miles in a year [1, 13]. When a company has millions of users then the company's need is that the game should be always up. So they quickly bring new versions of the game, which is not an easy task. As they have a very complicated environment because some users are an android user and some are ios users. Also, pokemon go has a gaming station so it has a very challenging environment to manage. All the gaming code of pokemon go is written in Java, and with that they use Hadoop. Their data is stored in the Google Big table. They create the container for the application to make it lightweight so that it can be easily accessible and easily deployed. So that more load can be managed by scaleup their containers and scale down when there is less load. The biggest challenge for niantic was horizontal scaling because they need a system to manage their load in the holiday season or when there is a heavy load. But, for pokemon Go vertical scaling was also

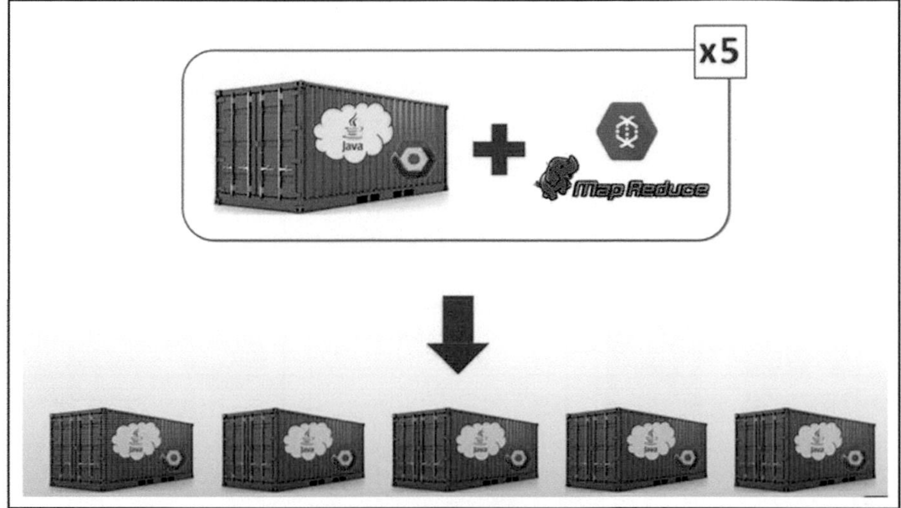


**Figure 9.6** Components used for high performance of containers.

a challenge. Horizontal scaling is when we add more nodes and in vertical scaling, we add more compute in the same node. So for managing the containers there was a need for a container orchestration tool. Hence, Kubernetes came into the picture. With the help of Kubernetes, they can handle as much as heavy load (Figure 9.6).

Before they were able to manage the traffic x5 times using the script or whatever method they used but after using Kubernetes they were able to handle x50 times traffic. Kubernetes helped them to auto-scale the containers to handle more traffic.

## 9.8 Kubernetes Architecture

The most basic Kubernetes architecture has two nodes (Figure 9.7)

- Master nodes
- Worker nodes

Let us firstly focus on what the worker nodes do.

### 9.8.1 Worker nodes

Most of the time we will be dealing with staff nodes, whether we have to uninstall the installed app or have to adjust it automatically, or have to

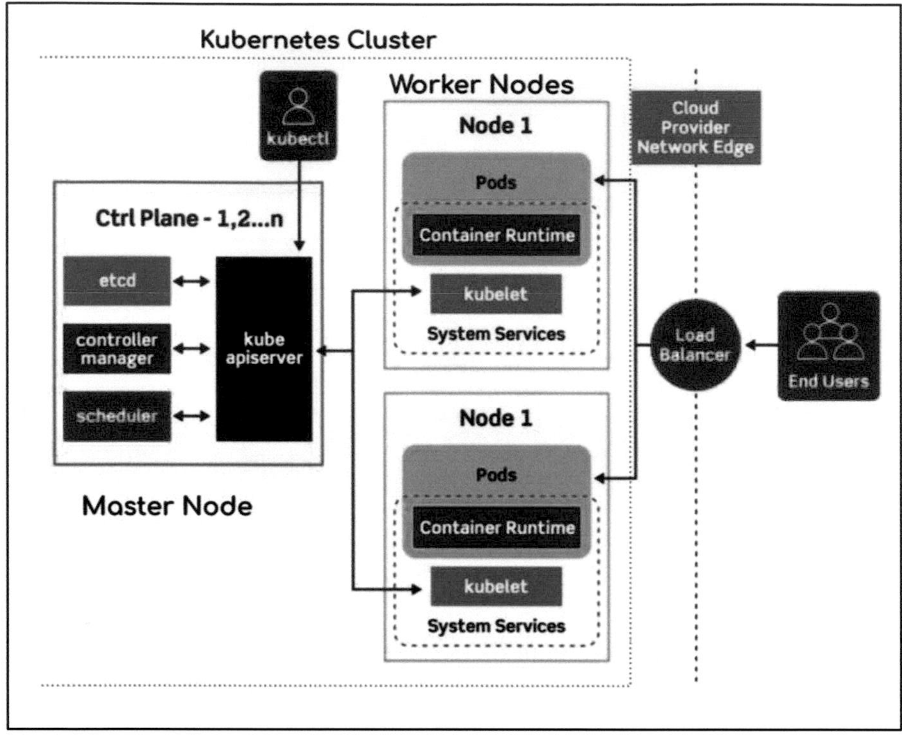


**Figure 9.7** Kubernetes ecosystem components.

uninstall any new app updates on the production-level server, it will usually handle staff nodes. As this node performs the actual function required by the cluster administrator or developer, it is known as the worker node. The employee node can have one or more pods, these pods are your application output installed in the container. Every function runs these three essential processes:

- Container Runtime
- kubelet
- kube-proxy

### 9.8.2 Container run time

Every Microservice (small app) feed module is packaged in a single pod with its own operating time. One needs to include the working time of the container in each employee area in the collection for the Pods to work there (Figure 9.8).

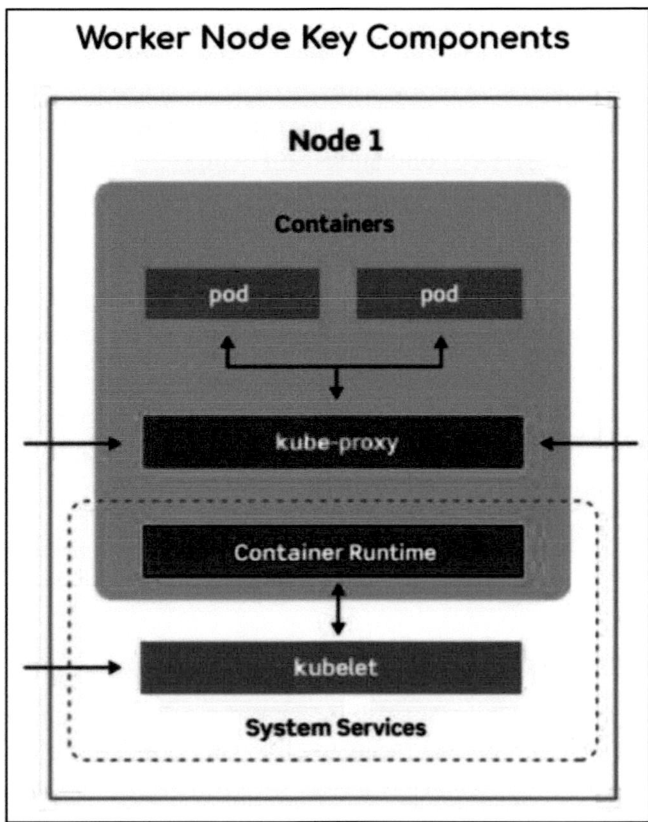


**Figure 9.8** Worker node structure.

### 9.8.3 Kubelet

Kubelet is the main agent of the employee node, interacting with both the node and the container in a given employee location. Kubelet is responsible to store a set of pods, built with one or more containers, in the local system, to register a node with the Kubernetes collection, post events and pod status, and report app usage.

### 9.8.4 Kube proxy

The K8s collection can have multiple user nodes and each node has multiple active pods, so if one has to access this pod, one can do so using Kube-proxy. Kube-proxy is a proxy network that works for each location in your collection, using part of the Kubernetes Service vision. To access the pod through k8s services, there are certain network policies, which allow network connectivity to your Pods from network sessions within or outside your collection. These rules are treated with proxy. Kube-proxy has a clever algorithm for forwarding the full network capacity required to access the pod which reduces overhead and makes service communication better.

### 9.8.5 Master node

A master node is also known as a control plane that is responsible for managing employee/slave premises properly. They work with the employee node to:

- Schedule
- Monitor the workers
- Start/restart
- Managing the new slave/worker nodes that are joining the Kubernetes cluster

### 9.8.6 Kubernetes control plane (AKA master node)

All Kubernetes items are recorded in a control system. Continuously monitors the object's conditions and reacts to changes in the kube-clusters; it also works to ensure that the system's real state matches the desired state. The control plane is made up of three primary pieces, as shown in the diagram above: the apiserver, the controller-manager, and the scheduler. To achieve the greatest availability, all of these can be used in one primary area or repeated over numerous critical nodes. API Server provides APIs for many sorts of applications to provide lifecycle orchestration (ratings, updates, and so on). It also serves as a gateway to the collection; therefore clients from outside the collection should be able to contact the API server. Clients communicate with an API server, which acts as a proxy for nodes and pods (and services). Metadata, such as labels and annotations, as well as the desired (specified) and target statuses, may be included in resources (current status). The controllers are working to get the real state to where they want it to be. Node status, autoscaling, storage (services and pods), service accounts, and tokens are all controlled by multiple controllers (word spaces). The control manager is a daemon that looks at a component's status and makes modifications to drive it to the desired position using key control loops. Cloud Management Manager connects to each cloud to provide complete support for available locations, virtual machine environments, storage resources, DNS network services, routing, and uploading (Figure 9.9).

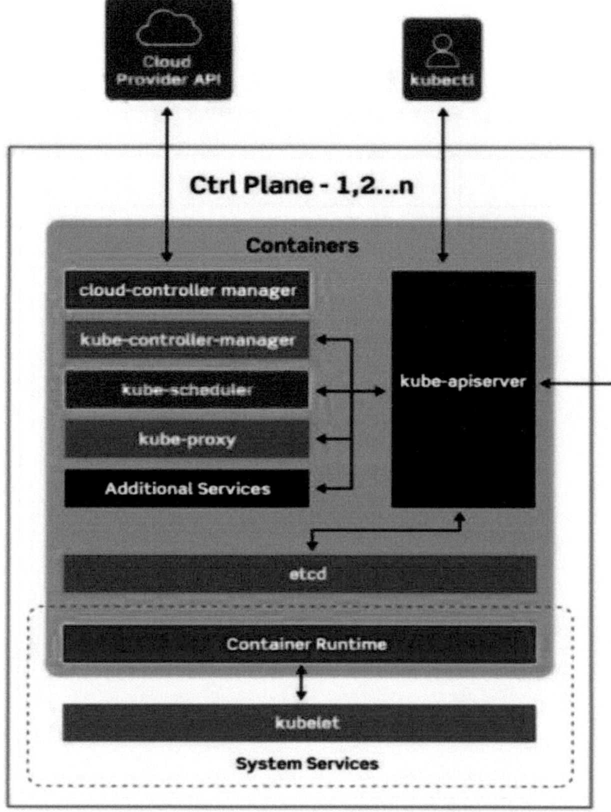


**Figure 9.9** AKA master node structure.

The Scheduler is responsible for arranging the containers for all nodes in the collection; considers various barriers, such as service limitations or guarantees, as well as specifications for compliance and contravention compliance.

### 9.8.7 Node

A node is a simple server or Virtual Machine instance, where our Kubernetes cluster or the application will be deployed and running. We can imagine it as a basic server where our product is deployed. These nodes can be increased or decreased according to the requirement or the flow of the traffic coming towards the application.

- A node can contain many pods (will be discussed in the following points).

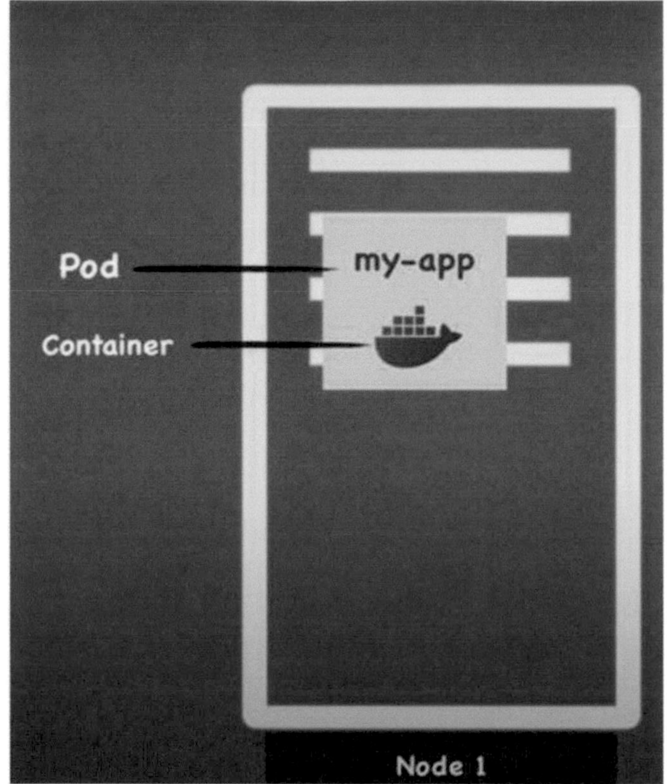


**Figure 9.10** POD structure.

- Kubernetes manages and handles the scaling of pods across nodes according to the need automatically in the cluster.
- A cluster can have one or many nodes.
- The architecture and other components that a node uses will be discussed in detail in the Kubernetes Architecture Section.

### 9.8.8 Pod

A pod is a basic unit or the smallest component of the Kubernetes cluster. It is basically an abstraction level above the Docker container (Figure 9.10).

- Pods contain the Docker containers.
- This is done to provide a run time environment for the containers and in this way, they can be managed easily by isolating each container into a pod.

- Each pod gets an IP address to communicate with other pods in that node.
- There is a catch here, whenever a POD is created it is assigned with a new IP, but if a pod dies and is recreated then it will again be assigned by a new IP address. This will be a headache to change the IP's everywhere to establish communication.
- To avoid this problem the service component is available in Kubernetes.

### 9.8.9 Service

This is a solution to the IP problem for pods. The service is such an IP address that remains without the relation of the POD life cycle. Even if the pod is restarted or newly created a service remains unchanged (Figure 9.11).

This gives the advantage of not changing the address every time. The main functionalities of the service are:

- Providing a permanent address.
- Acting as a Load Balancer.

#### 9.8.9.1 Internal service

This service can be used to make communication internally amongst the pods present in a node. This service is generally created to establish the connection between the application and the database where external users or modules must not access it.

#### 9.8.9.2 External service

This service is created to make the interaction and establish a connection between the application and the external users/modules. This generally is the address by which the browser reaches the application.

### 9.8.10 Ingress

Ingress acts as a before component of services. It is the first point of communication in the cluster. It further redirects to the services for information and network sharing. Allows us to combine our route rules into a single app as it can expose multiple applications under the same IP address.

### 9.8.11 ConfigMap

ConfigMap is an API object used to store non-confidential data in keyword pairs. Pods can use ConfigMaps as location variables, command line

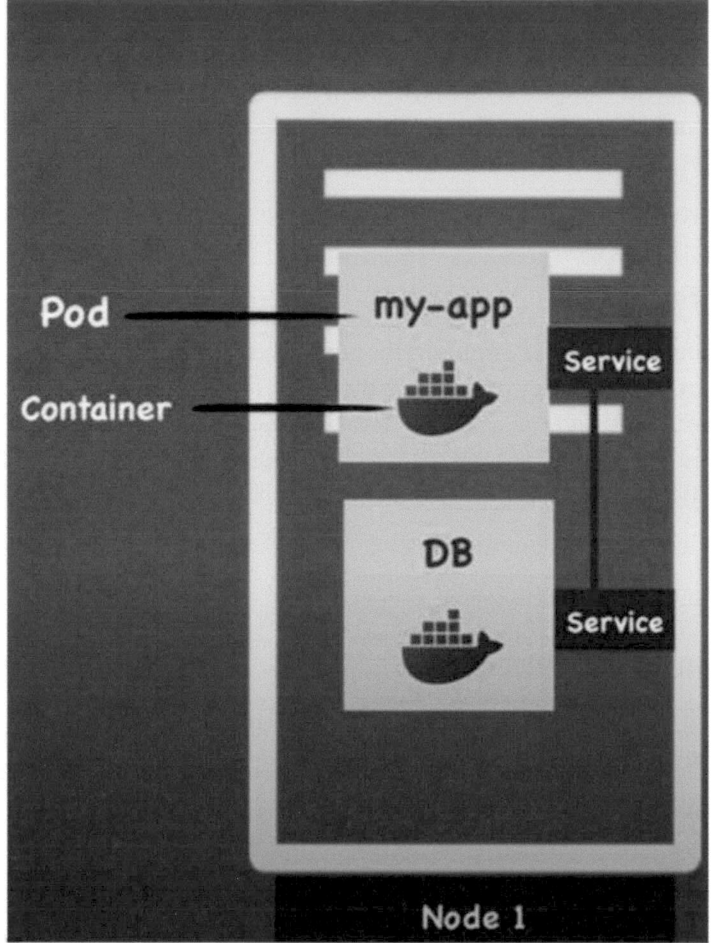


**Figure 9.11** POD service structure.

arguments, or volume configuration files. ConfigMap lets you separate location-specific configurations from your container images, making your applications more manageable. It can also be explained as an external configuration file, where we can specify all the configurations of the cluster and make changes easily, which will affect all areas where it is in use.

There are four different ways you can use ConfigMap to configure an internal Pod container:

- Inside the command of the container and the args
- The natural variables of the container

- Add the file with read volume only, so the program is readable
- Write the code that will work inside the Pod using the Kubernetes API to read ConfigMap

ConfigMaps can be installed as data volumes. For example, ConfigMaps can capture data that other parts of the system should use to repair.

The most common way to use ConfigMaps is to adjust the settings of the containers running on the Pod instead of the same names. You can also use ConfigMap separately.

### 9.8.12 Secret

A Secret is an item that contains a small amount of sensitive data such as a password, token, or key. Such information may be included in the Pod format or in the container image. Using Privacy means you do not need to encrypt private data in your app code. Because Secrets can be created independently without the Pods they use, there is a small risk that the Privacy (and its data) will be disclosed during creating, viewing, and editing Pods. Kubernetes, and applications that work in your collection, may also take additional security measures with Confidentiality, such as avoiding encrypting private data in a secure location.

It is similar to ConfigMap to save secret information such as credentials, usernames, passwords, keys, etc., that we want to be stored as configurations in an encoded manner.

### 9.8.13 Volume

Kubernetes supports many types of volumes. A pod can use any number of volume types simultaneously. If the pod is no longer available, Kubernetes destroys the premium volumes; Kubernetes, however, does not dispose of continuous scrolls. At any volume in the given pod, data is stored throughout the container restart. In its backbone, volume is an index, which may have some data on it, which is accessible to containers in the pod. How that catalog exists, the supporting medium, and its content are determined by the type of volume used. This volume can be a local volume inside the node or it can also be an external storage to backup all the data, frequently.

### 9.8.14 Deployments

It is used to tell K8s how to modify or create podcasts with a container application. Posting can measure the number of replica pods, enable updated code output, or revert to the previous feed version if needed. Kubernetes automatically performs repetitive tasks and manual tasks involved in extracting, measuring, and updating applications in production. We can replace broken pods or bypass the lower nodes, replacing those pods to maintain the continuity of key applications, because the Kubernetes deployment controller monitors the health of the pods and nodes in real time. Posting enables the automatic introduction of pod modes and ensures they work as defined across all nodes in the collection. Additional default translates to faster use with fewer errors. Posting is an easy way that measures the containers and applications work in a kubecluster, and open API makes integrations simple on CICD pipelines.

## 9.9 POD Lifecycle

Like individual application containers, Pods are considered to be almost ephemeral (rather than firm) commercial. Pods are created, assigned a unique ID (UID), and sorted into their living quarters until completed (under the policy of restart) or deleted. If a Node dies, the Pods are scheduled for that node which is scheduled to be removed after the closing time.

### 9.9.1 Waiting

If the container is not in a working or disconnected state, it is waiting. The standby mode is still using the functions we need to complete the launch: for example, dragging a container image to a container image text, or using private data. When we use kubectl to ask for a Pod with a Pending container, we also see the Reason field to summarise why the container is in that state.

### 9.9.2 Running

The operating condition indicates that the container is operating without problems. If there was a hook for postStart suspended, it was already done and completed. When we use kubectl to ask a Pod about an Active Container, we also see information about when a container has been in Active mode.

### 9.9.3 Terminated

The container in the Restricted container has been activated and is running out or failing for some reason. When you use kubectl to query a Pod with a Trimmed Container, you see the reason, the exit code, and the start and end time for that container use. If the container has a preStop hook set, which operates before the container enters Mode.

## 9.10 Conclusion

When we talk about the applications of Kubernetes in the industry, various tech giants such as Google, Spotify, Pinterest, Tinder, etc., have started to incorporate Kubernetes into the architecture since 2015, that is, when it was introduced as an open-source tool. One significant point is that Google has made more than nine lakh contributions to the open-source Kubernetes project, which is more than any of the companies to date. Google has also introduced GKE (Google Container Engine) through which we can deploy Kubernetes applications to the Google cloud, which was discussed at greater length in the above sections.

## References

[1] Claps, G. G., Svensson, R. B. and Aurum, A. On the journey to continuous deployment: Technical and social challenges along the way. Information and Software technology, 57 (2015), 21–31.

[2] Humble, J. and Molesky, J. Why enterprises must adopt devops to enable continuous delivery. Cutter IT Journal, 24, 8 (2011), 6.

[3] Pant, S., Kumar, A., Ram, M., Klochkov, Y., & Sharma, H. K. (2022). Consistency Indices in Analytic Hierarchy Process: A Review. Mathematics, 10(8), 1206.

[4] Sharma, H. K., Khanchi, I., Agarwal, N., Seth, P., & Ahlawat, P. (2019). Real time activity logger: A user activity detection system. *Int J Eng Adv Technol*, *9*(1), 1991–994..

[5] Khanchi, I., Ahmed, E., & Sharma, H. K. (2020, March). Automated framework for real-time sentiment analysis. In *5th International Conference on Next Generation Computing Technologies (NGCT-2019).*

[6] Sharma, H. K., Kumar, S., Dubey, S., & Gupta, P. (2015, March). Auto-selection and management of dynamic SGA parameters in RDBMS. In *2015 2nd International Conference on Computing for Sustainable Global Development (INDIACom)* (pp. 1763–1768). IEEE.

[7] Sharma, H. K., Singh, S. K., & Ahlawat, P. (2014). Model-based testing: the new revolution in software testing. *Database Syst J*, *4*(1), 26–31. Sharma, Hitesh Kumar, et al. "SGA Dynamic Parameters: The Core Components of Automated Database Tuning." Database Systems Journal 5.2 (2014): 13–21.

[8] Sharma, H. K., Shastri, A., Biswas, R., & Singh, S. K. (2014). SGA Dynamic Parameters: The Core Components of Automated Database Tuning. *Database Systems Journal*, *5*(2), 13–21.

[9] Dyck, A., Penners, R. and Lichter, H. Towards definitions for release engineering and DevOps. In Proceedings of the Proceedings of the Third International Workshop on Release Engineering (Florence, Italy, 2015). IEEE Press.

[10] Sharma, H. K., Jindal, M., Munjal, K., & Jain, A. (2017). An effective model of effort estimation for Cleanroom software development approach. *ICRDSTHM-17) Kuala Lumpur, Malasyia.*

[11] Kumar, A., Pant, S., Ram, M., & Yadav, O. (Eds.). (2022). Meta-heuristic Optimization Techniques: Applications in Engineering (Vol. 10). Walter de Gruyter GmbH & Co KG.

[12] Singh, H., Jatain, A., & Sharma, H. K. (2014). A review on search based software engineering. *IJRIT Int. J. Res. Inform. Technol*, *2*(4).

[13] Lwakatare, L. E., Kuvaja, P. and Oivo, M. Relationship of DevOps to Agile, Lean and Continuous Deployment: A Multivocal Literature Review Study. Springer, City, 2016.

# 10

# Containerisation Services on Cloud Computing Platforms


## Abstract

Cloud Computing is highly integrated with DevOps. For deployment and management of containers, cloud platforms and services are used. There are special services on cloud computing that are dedicated to containerization. It helps to smooth the transition and handling of microservices. In this chapter, we have explained the significance of cloud computing platforms for creating and managing container services.


## 10.1 Introduction

Virtual machines (VMs) are used by many large businesses to build a computerised computer environment. A virtual machine is a virtual computer simulation. VMs make it possible to run more than one operating system on one server. It is highly improving the utility of enterprise applications, wherein a software layer called hypervisor manages VMs. It separates VMs from each other and provides hardware resources for each VM. Each VM has direct or visual access to CPU, memory, storage and communication resources. Each virtual machine contains a complete operating system with related applications and libraries, known as the 'visitor' OS. There is no dependency between the VM and the host application, so Linux VMs can work on Windows machines, and vice versa [1, 2]. The container is a high-profile software part that packs code and all its dependencies so that the application can run shortly and securely from one computer location to a different computer location. For example, the Docker Container image is a very light, freestanding, user-friendly software package that covers all the essential things required to run an app like code, operating time, tools, libraries and system settings.

## 10.2 Containers in the Cloud

The images of a container become the container itself during operation and in the case of Docker, container images become containers when working with Docker Engine. Present on both Linux-based applications and Windows-based applications, the container-based software, did not affect by the infrastructure. They will work in the same way. Container detached the software, where it is present, and makes sure that it works the same despite the difference in platforms or any upgradation. The container is a high-grade software block that packs the code and all dependencies so that the application can work quickly and safely on one computer. For example, Docker Container Image is a lighting, autonomous user software package that includes code, open system tools, and settings to start the system libraries. The container image is a container during operation and the image becomes a container when you work on a Docker Engine for a Docker container. Linux applications and software for containers in Windows can be operated independently of the infrastructure. The container disconnects the software from its own place and ensures that it works even in the moderniser and the platform. Containers are the most significant part of the cloud environment. Most organisations are looking to containers as the second option to their preferred virtual machine (VM) for heavy-scale business operations [3]. Microservices container is simple and ideal for applications with embedded microservices that contain many standalone services that can be plugged in freely. There are many organisations where they are using more than one cloud location. In that case, containers are the best option for distributing workloads (Figure 10.1).

A fixture is one, which is easily transferable between the on-premises and public cloud data centres. An Announcement Upgrade is the most common way to upgrade an asset application to download a container and shift to the cloud as it is (a model known as 'lift and slide'). Most DevOps teams use microservices architectures to build applications and containers to discover resources. Containers are also utilised to provision and measure the DevOps architecture for example CI/CD tools [4]. There are some main reasons why containers provide compelling benefits compared to virtual machines:

**Microservices:** Containers are best suited for the construction of microservices, where applications are divided into smaller, more independent, non-distributed and individual components. Containers are an attractive option for sending and measuring each of those microservices.

**Multi-cloud:** Containers offer greater flexibility and versatility than VMs in cloudy environments. When software components are distributed in

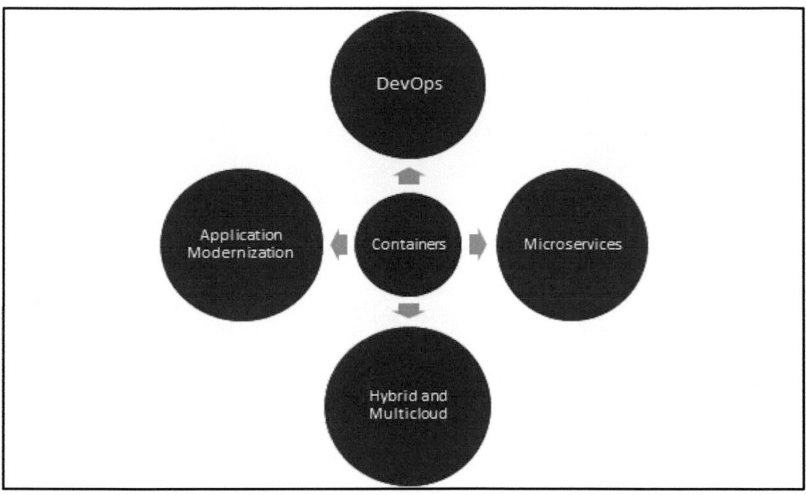


**Figure 10.1** Integration of container.

containers, it is possible to 'lift and move' those containers easily from empty metal servers, to existing locations, to public cloud sites.

**Automation:** Container is easily controlled by the API and is thus suitable for automation and Continuous Integration/Continuous Deployment (CI/CD).

## 10.3 Cloud-based Containers Working

The container is an ordinary choice for downloading and working software applications in the cloud server. Containers are comfortable to pull applications out of the visible area where they operate. The container packs all the software-related dependencies and uses it in a remote location (Figure 10.2).

Containers are the new technology, which partitioned sections and Chroot processes entered as a chunk of Linux. The new emerging container motor takes the application for installing the application (for example, a Docker) and a system container (for example, Linux Container). The container depends on the partition that can be used using control and application at the operating system kernel level [4, 5]. The container has a kernel for the OS and does not need to use the entire OS, so we must use only the files, libraries and configurations we need to use for the workload. The host operating system limits the ability of the container to use visual resources. General templates in the cloud are to use the container to start the application

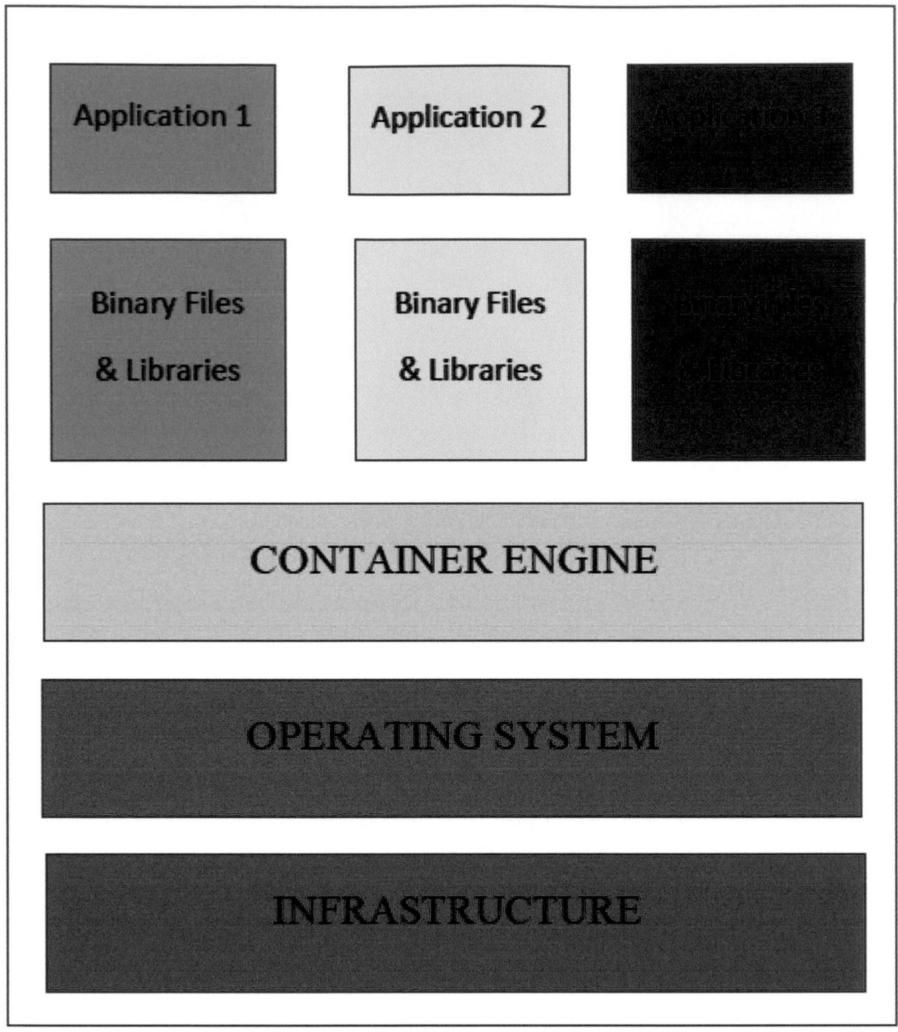


**Figure 10.2** Cloud-based container architecture.

event. It can be a background application similar to a website or part of a separate microservice or intermediate software. The container allows us to run multiple applications in a cloud virtual diet so that the problem of the container, which is failed, does not attack other containers or the entire virtual machine.

The vendor in the cloud provides different types of services that we can use to start the content of the cloud:

**Hosted container instances:** VM CLOUD, we can use the container directly with public cloud architecture, and does not require a Cloud Mediator. For example an Azure Container Instance (ACI) [6].

**Containers as a Service (CaaS):** Containers are generally in a tier, which has limited replay ability. Examples include Amazon Elastic Container Service (ECS) or Amazon Fargate.

**Kubernetes as a Service (KaaS):** Kubernetes is the most famous container orchestrator, regarding managing service. We can use container clusters in the public cloud. Google Kubernetes Engine (GKE) is an example.

## 10.4 Virtual Machines and Containers in a Cloud Environment

Cloud computing, the underlying appliance is given to provide the functionality of a virtual machine (VM). For example, containers and virtual machines (VMs) are non-dependent computer components. Unlike containers, virtual machines occupy a full Operating System to run an instance. VM can run as a guest OS other than the hosting machine on which it is running. If the host OS is windows, the VM can run a different OS like Linux. In most technology cases, virtual machines provide better separation and safety than containers. Since a virtual machine can be a separate machine with its own OS, it takes more time than Container to run. We can create different VMs from VM images but they are heavier than container images. There is one more disadvantage that VMs are very difficult to launch an instance automatically. Companies, which are providing cloud services, nowadays provide the service by which we can directly use containers on bare metal, except virtual machines as intermediaries, a model known as 'container instances'.

## 10.5 Bridging Containers and the Cloud: Challenges and Solutions

### 10.5.1 Migration

Migration of containers can significantly reduce costs, but it is very challenging to convert ongoing programs to containers on a typical computer system. In many organisations, IT staff need no knowledge of the ship and need training or help for coordinators. Cloud computing increases the technical work of many workgroups. Containers can add different levels of complexity. Changes in technical, organisational or professional groups must be adapted to traditional cloud technologies. Container ecosystems provide various types of tools which can easily open and includes services that guarantee fast travel and use.

### 10.5.2 Container security

The responsibility of the cloud suppliers is to protect the basic architecture and the responsibility of the customers is to properly configure the necessary security management elements that protect workload and the data features.

For containers, the cloud vendor takes the responsibility of the submoper vendor along with the hypervisor. However, the container storage volume must be protected by the organisation. Container protection includes several features.

- The container image can contain vulnerable components of software or malware.
- Automatic adjustment of engines such as Docker provides more rights. An attacker can use the kernel assigned to the host operating system as well as ongoing different containers and host OS if containers are not shut down appropriately.
- Containers have a short lifespan, making them very difficult to track, control and diagnose. Safety is important throughout the life of a vessel.

### 10.5.3 Container networking

Container networks are complex in nature, and this complexity leads to security concerns. You cannot use existing communication methods in your area with containers. The container network uses standards such as the interface of the container network interface (CNI) and is controlled by overlapping networks. Make a separate confidential network between containers and hosts. In the cloud, cloud providers face difficulties in providing contact names such as virtual private cloud (VPC) and security commands [7]. If you are using a private container in the cloud, you must manage your network and verify that it is compatible with the secrets you set in the public cloud. If you are wrong, you can ultimately expose a container on the public Internet.

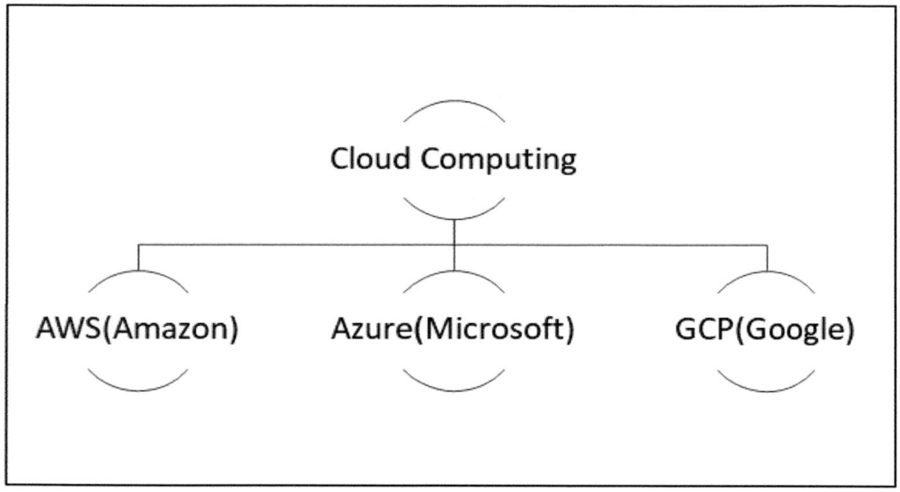


**Figure 10.3** Cloud platforms for containerisation.

## 10.6 Cloud Computing Platforms

In Figure 10.3, we have shown various cloud platforms used for containerisation.

- AWS by Amazon
- Azure by Microsoft
- GCP by Google

### 10.6.1 Amazon web services (AWS)

Amazon, a pioneer in cloud computing, was the first company to join the market for cloud services during the past ten years, earning itself several products and clients. AWS is now considered a standard for the excellence of cloud services. The infrastructural services (IaaS) list provided by AWS can be divided into categories for computers, websites, content distribution and storage, and networks. AWS uses non-server resources including Amazon Kinesis Streams, Amazon SQS Queues and AWS Lambda Functions to support the flow of seamless and flexible data collecting. It gives businesses the choice to choose an operating system, website, programming language, web application platform and other features based on their requirements. Utilising AWS management tools like AWS CloudTrail and Amazon CloudWatch to track user activity and AWS Config to manage resources and modifications. It is possible to monitor the use of cloud infrastructure services. Organisations' output and economic expansion are significantly improved by AWS [8]. Complex infrastructure and defined service restrictions established in line with the needs of all users are few obstacles to AWS. The largest of the three cloud providers' data centres, Amazon is spread over eighty-four different areas of the world.

### 10.6.2 Microsoft Azure

The goal of the Microsoft Azure Forum is to create, provide and oversee a wide range of services and applications using a vast network of Microsoft-owned data centres. Azure's product offerings span computer, network, data management and website capabilities. Organisations of all sizes can schedule domain and domain duplication as well as data capture on VMs hosted by Azure. Thanks to Azure Site Recovery. Zone redundant storage (ZRS) [9] or data storage for numerous data centre locations is offered by Azure. By enabling data centre communication with Azure through a private channel rather than the Internet, Azure ExpressRoute offers high security, high dependability and low latency. Azure also offers a wide range of communication features, such as support for visual networks across several sites and the ability to link virtual networks in various regions. Azure offers the most affordable necessary price and model costs. Professional engineers can use Azure Machine Learning Studio to create, test and implement algorithms.

### 10.6.3 Google cloud platform (GCP)

In April 2008, Google released the App Engine preview version, a developer tool that let users run their web applications on Google infrastructure. 'Make it simple to start with a new web app, and then make it simple to scale after that app has large traffic and millions of users', was the mission statement of App Engine.

GCP is an appealing alternative to AWS and Azure because of its precise visual interface, low price, adjustable settings and versatile machine possibilities. All data and communication links that mix traffic between data centres are completely encrypted by Google. Google Cloud and AWS compete head-to-head in several markets, including those that allow for flexible terms and payments, privacy and traffic security, cost reductions and machine learning. While all three cloud service providers provide discounts of up to 75% on warranties lasting one to three years, only Google further provides discounts of up to 30% on models with continuous consumption of more than 25% per month. The 12-month free GCP credit and a free timeline are equivalent to the 1-year free AWS trial. The GCP credit model [10] is ideal for businesses that have just started using cloud services. Google provides several pre-built APIs for translation, native language processing and computer vision. Machine learning engineers can create models based on TensorFlow's comprehensive reading library of Google Cloud Machine Learning Engine.

## 10.7 Amazon Web Services (AWS) Containerisation Service

AWS services, which are offered by Amazon, make advantage of an increased IT infrastructure to deliver critically important IT services. It offers a wide range of services, such as integrated software as a service (SaaS), platform as a service (PaaS) and infrastructure as a service (IaaS). AWS, a cloud computing platform that Amazon introduced, enables several enterprises to leverage dependable IT infrastructure.

- A small manufacturing company is using its technology to grow its business, leaving IT management in AWS.
- An international company could use AWS to provide training to deployed staff.
- The real estate company could use AWS to provide a more efficient computer delivery model.
- The media company uses AWS to provide various types of content for example ebox or audio files to global files.

**Pay-As-You-Go Service:** According to Pay-As-You-Go concept, AWS enables services to customers when needed without any prior appointment or advance investment. Pay-As-You-Go allows users to access AWS services (Figure 10.4):

- Computer
- Planning models
- Website maintenance
- Network

### 10.7.1 Benefits

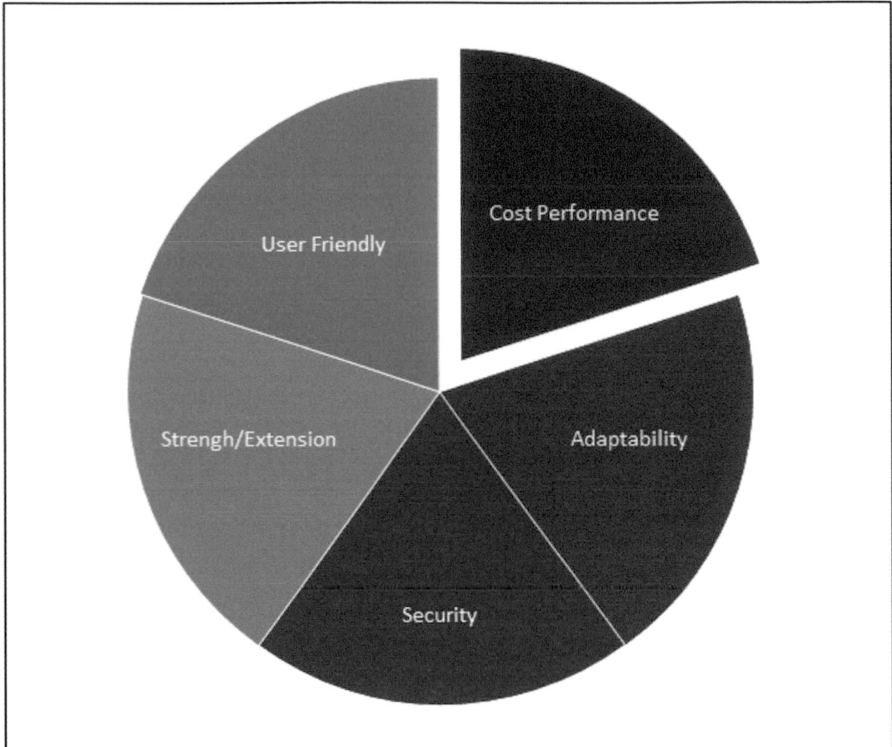


**Figure 10.4** Benefits of cloud-based containers.

#### 10.7.1.1 Adaptability

We may find more time than usual for core business activities due to the faster availability of new facilities and services in AWS. AWS Provides seamless hosting of legacy applications. There is no need for AWS to learn new technologies and software migration to AWS provides improved computer and efficient storage. AWS also extends the option of if we want to use the apps and services altogether or not. We may also prefer to use any part of the IT infrastructure in AWS and the remaining portion of the data centres (Figure 10.4).

#### 10.7.1.2 Cost performance

AWS does not require prior investment, long-term commitment and low cost compared to conventional IT infrastructure that requires significant investment.

#### 10.7.1.3 Strength/extension

With AWS, automatic measurement methods and load balancing methods are spontaneously lowered up or down, where asked increases or decreases accordingly. AWS strategies are well-suited for handling unexpected or extremely high loads. For this reason, organisations enjoy reduced cost benefits and increased user satisfaction.

#### 10.7.1.4 Security

AWS offers end-to-end protection and privacy for users. AWS is a visual structure that provides full access while managing complete privacy and segregation of its functions. Customers expect a high level of physical security due to Amazon's several years of experience in designing, maintaining and developing large IT operations centres. AWS guarantees three components of security, namely, Confidentiality, Integrity and User Data Access.

#### 10.7.1.5 User friendly

This is at the top of the list of Amazon Web Services advantages. AWS is simple to use because the infrastructure is specifically intended for fast and secure access. Users can make changes to their data whenever and anywhere they choose. Most businesses find that starting with AWS as their cloud provider is significantly easier than starting with Azure or Google Cloud Platform. AWS delivers all of the knowledge, documentation and video tutorials you need to understand how to use all of its services.

### 10.7.2 AWS global infrastructure

AWS is essentially a global cloud computing platform. Global infrastructure is a region where AWS has a presence. With plans to add 15 additional Availability Zones and 5 more AWS Regions in Canada, Israel, Malaysia, New Zealand, and Thailand, the AWS Cloud currently spans 99 Availability Zones throughout 31 geographical regions of the Globe (Figure 10.5).

The elements that make up the AWS infrastructure are as follows:

- Region
- Edge accommodation
- Regional edge warehouses

#### 10.7.2.1 Location available as a data centre

- Available location is an opportunity that can be found in the country or city. Within this opportunity, that is, data centre, may have multiple

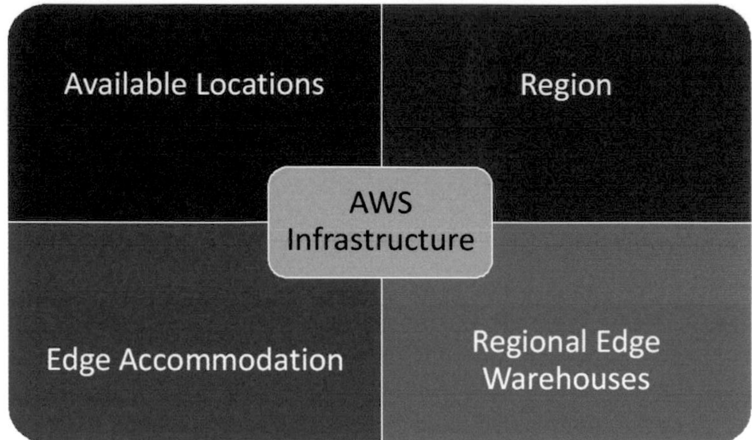


**Figure 10.5** AWS infrastructure.Available locations

servers, switching, load balancing, firewalls, etc. Cloud-related objects reside within the data centres.

- Available location may be a few data centres, but it is counted as 1 access point if they are close together.

#### 10.7.2.2 Region

- A region is a country. Each region has two more available areas.
- A regional set of data centres that is fully separated from other areas.
- A region contains more than two available locations connected to each other by links.

#### 10.7.2.3 Edge accommodation

- Edges AWS terminals are used to store content.
- Edge sites include CloudFront, Amazon's content delivery network (CDN).
- Edges are wider than regions. At present, there are more than 150 places on the edge.
- Edge area is not a small area that AWS has used to store content.
- Edge areas are mainly associated with many major cities to divide the content to users with reduced latency.

- For example, if another user accesses a website from Singapore, then the application will be redirected to a location near Singapore where the database is to be read.

#### 10.7.2.4 Regional edge cache

AWS announced a fresh remote location in November 2016, known as the Regional Edge Cache.

- Regional Edge storage is located between CloudFront Origin servers and peripherals.
- The regional edge has a larger archive than the single-edge archive.
- Data is archived in a remote location while data is stored in Regional Edge Caches.
- Data is no longer available remotely when a user requests data. Therefore, the terminal returns data stored in the regional boundary repository instead of the original servers with a maximum delay time.

### 10.7.3 Identity access management

Customers of Amazon Online Services (AWS) can manage users and their rights on AWS using the web service known as AWS Identity and Access Management. Organisations may manage users, security data like access keys, and permissions to limit which AWS resources users can access with IAM. Multi-user organisations must either share a safe security account or create numerous user accounts outside of IAM, each with their own memberships and subscriptions for AWS products. You also lack control over what users can do without IAM. IAM gives the company the ability to create several users, each with its own security details that are managed and charged to a single AWS account.

### 10.7.4 Features of identity access management

- **Internal account control:** One can manage the creation, revocation and rotation of each user's security information. Additionally, one may regulate who has access to what data and how in the AWS system.
- **Shared access to your AWS account:** Users can pool resources for collaborative projects.
- **Granular permissions:** These permissions can be adjusted so that every user can use a certain service but not others.

- **Identity federation:** IAM may be used with Facebook, Active Directory, LinkedIn and other services via the Identity Federation. Customers can use a username and password to sign in to the AWS Console just like they would with Facebook, Active Directory, etc.
- **Multiple items verification:** AWS gives more verification where we need to enter a user ID, password, etc., to access the AWS System.
- **Organisation-based permissions:** Users may be limited by AWS access based on their activities, for example, administrator, engineer and so on.
- **Network controls:** IAM guarantees that users can have the right to AWS services within the organisation's business network.
- **Give temporary rights to users/devices and services wherever required:** If we are accessing the mobile application and saving data in the AWS account, we can only perform this if we are using temporary access.
- **Includes many distinct AWS resources:** IAM is compiled with many distinct AWS facilities.
- **Lastly consistent:** The IAM service remains unchanged as it gains high usability by duplicating content across different servers in the Amazon data centre worldwide.

AWS container services make it easy to manage your basic infrastructure, whether locally or in the cloud, so we can focus on innovation and the needs of our business. About 80 percent of all cloud containers operating in AWS today. Customers like Samsung, Expedia, GoDaddy and Snap prefer to use their containers on AWS for security, reliability and growth. Container management tools can be divided into three categories: registration, singing and counting. AWS provides services that provide us with a secure place to store and manage our container images. The orchestration controls when and where your containers operate and have flexible computer engines to power your containers. AWS can help manage our containers and shipping, so we do not have to think about basic infrastructure. No matter what we build, AWS makes it easy and efficient to build with containers.

## 10.8 Amazon Elastic Container Service (Amazon ECS)

A very quick container management service is Amazon ECS. It allows us to launch, set up and control containers within the collection. Your containers with Amazon ECS are described by the function you employ to carry out particular tasks or jobs within the service. The service in this instance is a setting, you may use to launch and maintain a specific number of jobs from the collection at once. On the server-free infrastructure provided by AWS Fargate, operations and services can be launched. As an alternative, you can start your own operations and services in the Amazon EC2 configuration settings. You own to have more control over your infrastructure.

Amazon ECS offers the following features:

- Server option with AWS Fargate. With AWS Fargate, you do not need to manage servers, manage power settings, or split container operating loads for your own protection. Fargate manages the infrastructure to manage your work infrastructure. You can customise the placement of your containers throughout your collection based on your application requirements, isolation policies and availability requirements.
- You can grant granular permissions for each of your containers. This allows for a high degree of isolation when building your apps. In other words, you can launch your containers with the security and compliance levels that you expect from AWS.
- Container orchestration is owned by AWS. As a fully managed service, Amazon ECS comes with AWS configuration and built-in best practices. This also means you do not need to manage control planes, nodes, or add-ons.

Continuous integration and continuous transmission (CI/CD). This is a standard procedure for microservice architectures based on Docker containers. You can build a CI/CD pipe that takes the following steps.

- Monitors change the location of the source code.
- Update your Amazon ECS services to deploy the updated image to your application.
- Create a new Docker image from that source. Pursue an image to a picture repository like Amazon ECR or Docker Hub. This plays a significant role in service-oriented structures and massively distributed programmes.
- Your microservice components are automatically recognised by service access as they are generated and disconnected from a particular infrastructure.

- Assistance in sending data from your model logs to CloudWatch Logs. You may check the logs of your container status in one handy spot after sending this information to Amazon CloudWatch. As a result, your container cases' disc space is not taken up by your container logs.
- The roadmap contains information about what teams are doing and allows AWS customers to provide direct feedback.

### 10.8.1 ECS terminology

- **Job description:** This is a plan that explains how the docker container should be presented. Once we get used to AWS, which is similar to LaunchConfig with the only difference that the dock instead of an example, includes context such as a portable hole, docker image and so on.
- **Function:** A functional box with context declared in Task Declaration. It can be considered as an 'example' of a Job Description.
- **Service:** Specifies the ongoing operations associated with a given Task Definition. This may involve a single operating container or a number of them, each using the same Job Description.
- **Cluster:** A logical collection of EC2 conditions. The model is registered in the ECS Cluster when an event installs the ecs-agent programme on the server. The ECS CLUSTER variable setting in /etc/ecs/ecs.config makes it simple to fix this.
- **Container instance:** This is merely an illustration of an EC2 instance running Docker and the ECS agent as part of the ECS Cluster.

### 10.8.2 Types of startups

There are two models you can use to use your containers:

- **Fargate launch type:** This is a pay-as-you-go option with no server. You can manage containers without the need to manage your infrastructure.
- **EC2 startup type**: Prepare and use EC2 conditions in your collection to use your containers.

The Fargate launch type is suitable for the following functions:

- Heavy workloads that need to be prepared for low-level work
- Occasionally small jobs that explode from time to time

- Small jobs
- Lots of work

The EC2 startup type is suitable for the following functions:

- Workloads that require high-density CPU and memory usage
- Major projects that need to be upgraded for a price
- Your apps need access to continuous storage

You must manage your infrastructure directly

## 10.9 Microsoft Azure Containerisation Services

In order to manage Microsoft's data centres' cloud services, Microsoft Azure was first introduced in 2008. In addition, to support multilingual programming languages, tools and frameworks, including Microsoft-specific and third-party ones, it offers software as a service (SaaS), platform as a service (PaaS) and infrastructure as a service (IaaS). Under the project code 'Project Red Dog', Azure was initially presented at Microsoft's Professional Developers Conference (PDC) in October 2008. It was subsequently released in February 2010 as Windows Azure and changed its name to Microsoft Azure on March 25, 2014. More than 200 products and cloud services are available on the Azure Cloud Platform, which is built to support your ability to innovate and meet today's problems. Build, deploy and manage applications with tools and frameworks of your choice across a variety of cloud, backyards and edges. Just as the transportation industry uses virtual containers to sort different loads to be transported on ships and trains, software development methods are increasingly using a method known as containerisation. A container is a standard software package that combines the application code with the necessary configuration files and libraries, as well as the dependencies required for the application to run. This empowers engineers and IT professionals to use applications across applications seamlessly. This allows the user to work with the system and its dependencies using separate app processes. Application code can be grouped by configuration and dependency. Developers can quickly and safely create and deploy apps thanks to containerisation. The code must be written to a specified computer location using traditional methods, which might occasionally result in mistakes when the code is transferred to another site. For instance, an engineer might move code from a desktop computer to a virtual machine (VM) or from the Linux operating system to the Windows one. This issue is resolved by containerisation, which

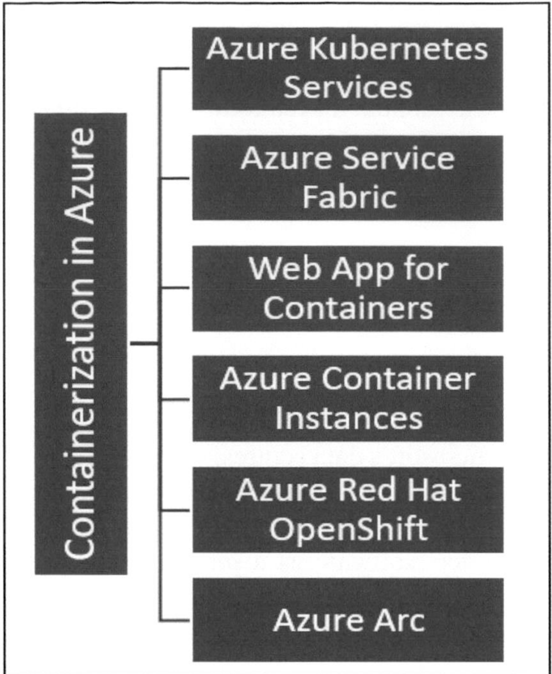


**Figure 10.6** Azure-based containerisation.

combines the application code with the required configuration data, libraries and dependencies. This single software package, or "container," is decoupled from the host operating system, enabling it to operate independently and portably across any platform or cloud without encountering any issues. The Azure containerisation system ranges from PaaS Services and IaaS services. For the sake of understanding azure containerisation services and platforms can be classified as follows (Figure 10.6):

### 10.9.1 Azure Kubernetes services (AKS)

Kubernetes is a container and cluster management solution, which is also known as an orchestration system. AKS is a Microsoft-managed Kubernetes service that lowers cluster configuration overhead and integrates functionality like identity, networking and monitoring. Kubernetes is now largely regarded as the container orchestration industry standard. The flexibility, automation and diminished administrative overhead for administrators and developers are the main advantages of AKS. For instance, AKS configures all of the Kubernetes nodes that manage and control the worker nodes during deployment on its own, in addition to performing several other tasks like integrating Azure active directory (AD), connecting to monitoring services and configuring advanced networking features like HTTP application routing. Users of Azure Monitor have the option of simultaneously monitoring all clusters or just one.

#### 10.9.1.2 Azure service fabric (ASF)

As a platform service, Azure Service Fabric is a proprietary Microsoft stack that includes its own development framework, tools, scalability and cluster management. Azure Service Fabric is able to run guest executables alongside containers. It was initially acquainted with giving a stage to modernising windows .NET applications in azure. With competing services now supporting Windows containers, Service Fabric's use for small- to medium-sized workloads is debatable.

#### 10.9.1.3 Web app for containers

You may use Azure App Service to run your custom docker image and make use of the managed platform service by using a web app for containers. You won't have to patch or deploy virtual machines, and you will be able to take advantage of App Service capabilities like auto-scaling, Azure Active Directory integration and custom domains.

#### 10.9.1.4 Azure container instances (ACI)

Azure container instances (ACI) is based on consumption rather than any virtual machines which make it a serverless offering. It is intended to be a simple and quick method to get started with containers, with no underlying virtual machines to handle. In order to form the foundation of a serverless cluster within AKS, ACI also provides 'virtual nodes'.

#### 10.9.1.5 Azure Red Hat Openshift

Microsoft and Red Hat collaborate to provide highly available, fully managed OpenShift clusters on demand using Azure Red Hat OpenShift. Red Hat OpenShift is built on Kubernetes. OpenShift is a turnkey container platform as a service (PaaS) with a greatly improved developer and operator experience as it brings added-value features to assist Kubernetes

#### 10.9.1.6 Azure Arc

A centralised management solution for on-premises servers, data services and Kubernetes clusters deployed in multicloud environments, Azure Arc is built on Azure. Several well-known Kubernetes distributions that have been approved by the Cloud Native Computing Foundation are supported by Azure Arc-enabled Kubernetes clusters (CNCF). The service connects with Azure management tools like Azure Policy and Azure Monitor and lets you list Kubernetes clusters in Azure across various settings for a consistent view (Figure 10.7).

### 10.9.2 Advantages of Azure containerisation services

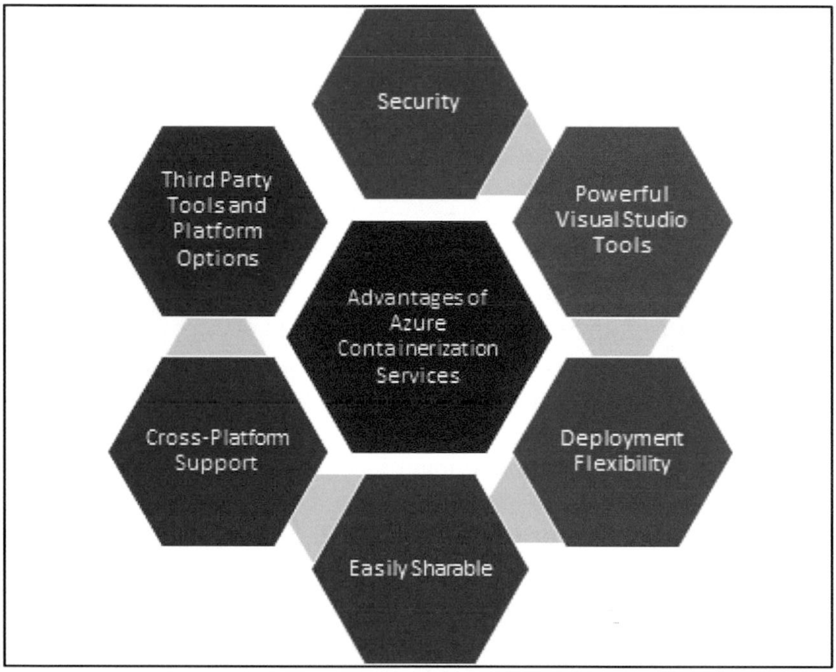

**Figure 10.7** Advantages of Azure-based cloud containerisation.

#### 10.9.2.1 Security

Microsoft has worked hard in recent years to provide first-rate features for monitoring, managing, and securing your containers in Azure. It offers Azure Container Registry, a Docker private registry, to let you manage your container images efficiently using well-known open-source Docker command line interface tools. It provides full-stack security capabilities like runtime protection, vulnerability scanning and Twislock or Aqua compliance. Enterprises may also incorporate Azure Active Directory into the application to enable single sign-on capabilities. Azure development specialists may receive a 360-degree view of the container environment, including memory, storage, centralised CPU, performance metrics and network, using tools such as Log Analytics and Application Insights (Figure 10.7).

#### 10.9.2.2 Powerful Visual Studio Tools

Visual Studio Tools for Docker are powerful tools for swiftly developing, deploying and debugging containerised applications. Developing .NET Core applications for Linux or.NET applications for Windows is simple. Our Azure developers can easily integrate containers into current DevOps workflows and swiftly iterate or debug multi-container-based apps using Visual Studio Team Services.

#### 10.9.2.3 Deployment flexibility

Use Azure compute services such as App Service, Azure Container Service (ACS) and Service Fabric to orchestrate and scale up and down your containers.

#### 10.9.2.4 Easily sharable

Push your Docker images to an Azure registry with ease; they may then be shared as pre-built container images in the future.

#### 10.9.2.5 Cross-platform support

You can deploy your containerised application in your own data centre, Azure stack, or Azure, resulting in a unified approach to building applications that can run on-premises or in the cloud.

#### 10.9.2.6 Third-party tools and platform options

Third-party solutions such as OpenShift, Docker Enterprise Edition and Pivotal Cloud Foundry make it simple to deploy containerised apps in Azure.

### 10.9.3 Use cases of Azure containerisation services

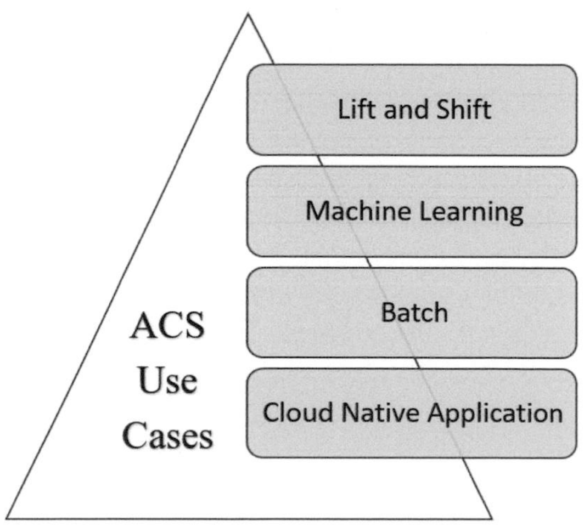


**Figure 10.8** Azure containers usage.

#### 10.9.3.1 Lift and shift

There are various advantages to moving to the cloud, but having to update old programmes is inconvenient and a major hurdle for many. Enterprises can theoretically transfer entire apps to the cloud using containers without changing any code (Figure 10.8).

#### 10.9.3.2 Machine learning

Containers make machine learning tools and apps self-contained and scalable in any environment.

#### 10.9.3.3 Batch

Batch processing usually refers to tasks that can be completed without the need for human interaction or on a resource-available basis. Images can be resized, reports can be generated, and data can be converted from one format to another. Containers make it simple to perform batch jobs without having to worry about managing an environment or dependencies.

#### 10.9.3.4 Cloud-native applications

Containers provide a standard operational architecture for cloud-native applications in a variety of settings, including public, private and hybrid. Containers are great for providing cloud-native apps because of their cheap overhead and high density.

## 10.10 Conclusion

Software management and download in the cloud can frequently be done using containers. Applications can be removed from the visible area where they operate using containers. All the software-related requirements are packed inside the container, which is then used in a distant place. Applications can be applied equally to any place, whether it is a public cloud, a private cloud, or an empty metal machine, with containers, which commonly employ the Docker container engine. Moving container programmes to the cloud is simple. Additionally, containers make it simple to access the cloud's most potent capabilities, which may be quickly deployed, integrated or optimised via APIs made available by the container engine/orchestrator.

## References

[1] Runeson, P. and Höst, M. Guidelines for conducting and reporting case study research in software engineering. Empirical software engineering,

14, 2 (2009), 131. Pant, S., Kumar, A., Ram, M., Klochkov, Y., & Sharma, H. K. (2022). Consistency Indices in Analytic Hierarchy Process: A Review. Mathematics, 10(8), 1206.

[2] Claps, G. G., Svensson, R. B. and Aurum, A. On the journey to continuous deployment: Technical and social challenges along the way. Information and Software technology, 57 (2015), 21–31.

[3] Hitesh Kumar Sharma; Anuj Kumar; Sangeeta Pant; Mangey Ram, "9 Methodologies for Improving the Quality of Service and Safety of Smart Healthcare," in Artificial Intelligence, Blockchain and IoT for Smart Healthcare , River Publishers, 2022, pp. 85–94.

[4] Hitesh Kumar Sharma; Anuj Kumar; Sangeeta Pant; Mangey Ram, "10 Cloud Commuting Platform for Smart Healthcare and Telemedicine," in Artificial Intelligence, Blockchain and IoT for Smart Healthcare , River Publishers, 2022, pp. 95–104.

[5] Hitesh Kumar Sharma; Anuj Kumar; Sangeeta Pant; Mangey Ram, "11 Smart Healthcare and Telemedicine Systems: Present and Future Applications," in Artificial Intelligence, Blockchain and IoT for Smart Healthcare , River Publishers, 2022, pp. 105–116.

[6] Sharma, H. K., Kumar, S., Dubey, S., & Gupta, P. (2015, March). Auto-selection and management of dynamic SGA parameters in RDBMS. In *2015 2nd International Conference on Computing for Sustainable Global Development (INDIACom)* (pp. 1763–1768). IEEE.

[7] Sharma, H. K., Jindal, M., Munjal, K., & Jain, A. (2017). An effective model of effort estimation for Cleanroom software development approach. *ICRDSTHM-17) Kuala Lumpur, Malasyia.*

[8] Kumar, A., Pant, S., Ram, M., & Yadav, O. (Eds.). (2022). Meta-heuristic Optimization Techniques: Applications in Engineering (Vol. 10). Walter de Gruyter GmbH & Co KG.

[9] Singh, H., Jatain, A., & Sharma, H. K. (2014). A review on search based software engineering. *IJRIT Int. J. Res. Inform. Technol*, *2*(4).

[10] Eck, A., Uebernickel, F. and Brenner, W. Fit for continuous integration: How organizations assimilate an agile practice (2014).

# Index

# About the Authors

**Hitesh Kumar Sharma** is working as an Associate Professor at the School of Computer Science, University of Petroleum and Energy Studies, Dehradun, Uttarakhand, India. He did his PhD in Database Performance Tuning in 2016. He completed his MTech in 2009. Currently, he is also working in Machine Learning, Deep Learning, Image Processing and IoT with Blockchain. He has authored more than 70 research articles in various journals and participated in conferences of national and international repute. Dr Sharma has authored three books and numerous book chapters with various international publishers. He is an active Guest Editor/Reviewer of various referred International journals. He has delivered various Keynotes/Guest speeches in India and abroad. He got many certifications in DevOps in the last two years. He has also published 03 Patents in his academic career in the last few years.

**Anuj Kumar** is an Associate Professor of Mathematics at the University of Petroleum and Energy Studies (UPES), Dehradun, India. Before joining UPES, he worked as an Assistant Professor (Mathematics) at the ICFAI University, Dehradun, India. He has obtained his Master's and doctorate degrees in Mathematics from G. B. Pant University of Agriculture and Technology, Pantnagar, India. His area of interest is reliability analysis, optimisation, MCDM and artificial intelligence. He has published many research articles in journals of national and international repute. He is an Associate Editor of the International Journal of Mathematical, Engineering and Management Sciences. He is also a regular reviewer of various reputed journals of Elsevier, IEEE, Springer, Taylor & Francis and Emerald.

**Sangeeta Pant** received her doctorate from G. B. Pant University of Agriculture and Technology, Pantnagar, India. Presently, she is working with the Department of Mathematics, School of Engineering and Computing, Dev Bhoomi Uttarakhand University, Dehradun, as an Associate Professor. Prior to it, she worked as an Assistant Professor SG (Mathematics) at the University of Petroleum and Energy Studies, Dehradun, India. She has published around 45 research articles in journals/books of national/international repute in her area of interest and is instrumental in various other research-related activities like editing/reviewing for various reputed journals and organising/participating in conferences. Her area of interest is numerical optimization, artificial intelligence, nature-inspired algorithms and multi-criteria decision-making.

**Mangey Ram** received the Ph.D. degree major in Mathematics and minor in Computer Science from G. B. Pant University of Agriculture and Technology, Pantnagar, India in 2008. He has been a Faculty Member for around fifteen years and has taught several core courses in pure and applied mathematics at undergraduate, postgraduate, and doctorate levels. He is currently the *Research Professor* at Graphic Era (Deemed to be University), Dehradun, India. Before joining the Graphic Era, he was a Deputy Manager (Probationary Officer) with Syndicate Bank for a short period. He is Editor-in-Chief of the *International Journal of Mathematical, Engineering and Management Sciences*; *Journal of Reliability and Statistical Studies*; *Journal of Graphic Era University*; Series Editor of six Book Series with *Elsevier*, *CRC Press-A Taylor and Frances Group*, *Walter De Gruyter Publisher Germany, River Publisher* and the Guest Editor & Associate Editor with various journals. He has published 400 plus publications (journal articles/books/book chapters/conference articles) in *IEEE, Taylor & Francis, Springer Nature, Elsevier, Emerald, World Scientific* and many other national and international journals and conferences. Also, he has published more than 60 books (authored/edited) with international publishers like *Elsevier*, *Springer Nature*, *CRC Press-A Taylor and Frances Group*, *Walter De Gruyter Publisher Germany, River Publisher*. His fields of research are reliability theory and applied mathematics. Dr. Ram is a Senior Member of the IEEE, the Senior Life Member of the Operational Research Society of India, the Society for Reliability Engineering, Quality and Operations Management in India, Indian Society of Industrial and Applied Mathematics, He has been a member of the organizing committee of a number of international and national conferences, seminars, and workshops. He has been conferred with the "*Young Scientist Award*" by the Uttarakhand State Council for Science and Technology, Dehradun, in 2009. He has been awarded the "*Best Faculty Award*" in 2011; the "Research Excellence Award" in 2015; "*Outstanding Researcher Award*" in 2018 for his significant contribution to academics and research at Graphic Era Deemed to be University, Dehradun, India. Also, he has received the "*Excellence in Research of the Year-2021 Award*" by the Honourable Chief Minister of Uttarakhand State, India, and the "Emerging Mathematician of Uttarakhand" state award by the Director, Uttarakhand Higher Education. Recently, he received the "*Distinguished Service Award-2023*" for the subject & nation development by Vijñāna Parishad of India.